Preparing for
Dressage the right way

Katja von Rönne

The correct training methods for success

Preparing for Dressage the right way

Katja von Rönne

The correct training methods for success

Impressum

Copyright © 2011 Cadmos Publishing Limited, Richmond, UK
Copyright of original edition © 2010 Cadmos Verlag GmbH, Schwarzenbek, Germany
Design: Ravenstein + Partner, Verden
Setting: Das Agenturhaus, Munich
Cover photograph: JB Tierfoto, Marschacht
Content photos unless otherwise indicated: JB Tierfoto, Marschacht
Translation: Claire Williams
Editorial of the original edition: Carmen Echelmeyer
Editorial of this edition: Karin Saxe
Printed by: Grafisches Centrum Cuno, Calbe

British Library Cataloguing in Publication Data
A catalogue record of this book is available from the British Library.

Printed in Germany

ISBN 978-0-85788-005-5

Contents

Introduction

The gap between theory and practice in riding can only be narrowed by building greater understanding and respect between horse and rider. In doing this, however, the ability to communicate on the same level and the "language" between the two is exceptionally important. The rider's aids form an important part of this language and are developed and refined over many years. Besides performing the technical elements of the required movements, this also involves the development of a "thinking rider", who works to train his horse with his body, mind and soul. It may take years of experience of mutual respect and trust until a rider learns to understand a horse within seconds – and vice versa. My intention with this book is to put together a schooling programme based on dressage work that has been correctly and systematically trained. I use a wide range of exercises and movements with a multitude of variations possible which enable me to put together individual

programmes. The exercises are arranged in a logical sequence so as to build on the work of the previous lessons. All riders will be able to put together an appropriate and creative training programme that suits both themselves and their horses.

But first you need understand what I mean when talking about "correct" dressage training. By this I mean training that is stress-free and that enables the horse to move under the rider with suppleness, enjoyment and ease, without tiring or unnecessary wear and tear on the horse's joints or, indeed, its health. To do this we need to supple the horse using classical methods beginning with basic exercises and building up to the "crowning glory" of collection. By the end of a horse's training it should respond to the smallest of signals from the rider to complete the required movements. The deeper you immerse yourself in the subject of riding, the clearer the complexity of

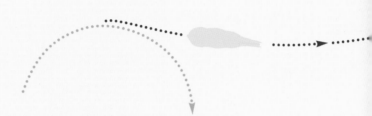

these connections become. The aim of training horse and rider is to awake an awareness of what it feels like when the movements are executed correctly, to learn how to do this and then apply this knowledge with less and less effort, in other words, with increasingly finer aids. The schooling exercises used for dressage training will become "old friends". They offer a sense of security and routine.

Every rider, riding instructor and trainer can use this knowledge for themselves and integrate it into their own daily routine. Whether training my own horses or teaching others, I am always being confronted with the same recurring problems. To overcome them I have developed a system using very similar or even the same series of exercises, that concentrate on elements of basic schooling: regularity, a feeling of rhythm, suppleness (the German term is Losgelassenheit, for which there is no equivalent expression in English. The meaning is a combination of suppleness, looseness and relaxedness), a swinging back, contact, appropriate degree of tension through the horse's body (the German term Körperspannung means literally body tension and is used in a positive sense and is a requirement for the successful completion of many exercises), as well as the appropriate preparation and development for the collected work. The successes of my pupils show me how effectively this system works.

Furthermore, it has also shown that "homework", comprising of a series of exercises based on the preceding lesson, gives excellent results. If the homework is understood, repeated daily and practised, then the horse and rider will make steady progress and what has been taught will really become well established.

This book as a whole forms an established training programme that has been proven to work. It is divided into three parts, each methodically building on what has gone before. The movements and exercises detailed focus on the basic principles of the Scales of Training (from the German Equestrian Federation). These are set out from easy to hard, from the known to the unknown. In addition, all of the exercises are connected to each other like a spider's web, and complement each other. While the first part concentrates on the basics, consisting of gaining a sense of balance, controlling rhythm and improving suppleness, the second part deals with containing the horse and starting to work towards collection. Providing that the preparatory work has been done, the movements that are introduced in the final and third part should "fall into your lap like ripe fruit" and are only broadly sketched out. To detail them in the same way as the other exercises it would be necessary to considerably expand the size of this book! The way the training programme is laid out makes it the easiest and at the same time healthiest and shortest way to train for dressage success.

As new exercises and movements are added to the basic exercises and schooling patterns used on a daily basis, the older ones serve as a foundation and should be regularly repeated. This helps to identify at an early stage any warning signs given out by your horse and gives you every opportunity to correct problems. Certain habits can creep in that you may not immediately notice, such as swishing of the tail, stubbornness, an unmotivated expression, nervousness, extreme tension or grinding of teeth. When training our horses it is our responsibility to identify these signs early and find a solution so that what starts as a little quirk doesn't become a annoying habit. To make the decision as to whether a horse can't or won't do what is being asked of it requires constant effort, a lot of time and experience. Throughout all of this riders will develop their own style of riding and will find themselves on a path starting from just learning to ride an exercise through to performing a movement with horse and rider working as a team, which, as a result of the ease and enjoyment with which it is done, can truly be described as a partnership.

As reader of this book, this means that if you are having problems at a certain stage of your training, and you aren't sure what has gone wrong, then flick back a few pages and check what the criteria are for that stage of training. Every chapter builds on the one before, which results in a logical structure for the entire training programme and for the individual sessions. It is important that you work in a methodical way as it forms a solid foundation for a long and healthy life for both horse and rider. The final part of the book gives an example of a training programme which you can use to create your own hourly, weekly and monthly plan. I always recommend that you create a training book in which you can record on a daily basis

a) Your aims.

b) What has actually been learned.

c) What happened and the results.

Every single step taken, even if only small, in the right direction when training will bring us closer to our final goal. Parallel to this, though, a knowledgeable trainer, working consistently and with a good eye, can help enormously through instruction, checking what you are doing and with feedback. The more you immerse yourself in your horse's training, the more exciting it becomes and shows you how much riding really is a never-ending story.

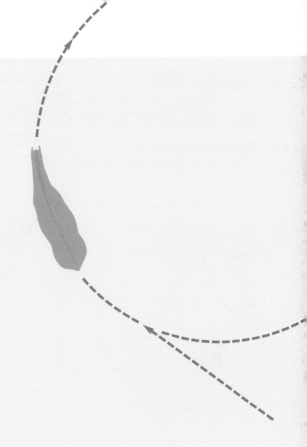

The basics

The easiest but most important first of all: the schooling of any horse starts with the basics. They are crucial for the effective suppling of the horse and its training throughout the horse's entire life. Once the basic foundations have been well established for both horse and rider , then it is relatively easy to start to build the "house" on it, in other words, to start to develop the more difficult movements on this foundation. A correctly built foundation is never wasted, and lasts a lifetime – even after breaks or time out for illness or injury. The more well established a horse is, in responding to the basic aids and the more positive his training has been, then the faster and easier it is to advance its schooling. No time spent on the basics is ever wasted, in fact, quite the opposite, as it creates the best possible psychological and physical state in a horse for its future. It is the foundation on which we can build.

Time and again I see horses that are brought to me after a long break and which are causing their riders real problems, since they aren't working like they did before. These difficulties are usually quite understandable, since often the horse's entire musculature has to be retrained. I worked with an eight-year-old chestnut that, following month-long lameness, had difficulty stretching down into the hand. The only pace that he could go in even a half-way relaxed manner was canter, which he was well suited to. In canter he could find his own rhythm and scored well because of his uphill movement. Considering its natural balance at this pace and its regular rhythm he found it easy to let his neck drop forwards and down from his withers. Building on this and within a fairly short period of time he was able to work better over his back, which was noticeably strengthened by the right muscles being worked. The strong connection resulting

Working the horse in a longer outline strengthens its back and helps to warm the horse up at the start of a lesson.

from this between his back and hind quarters made the progression into collected work possible without the loss of any more time. To reach this stage with a horse following a lengthy illness I would normally require four weeks.

In the case of every horse you need to climb the training ladder rung by rung. If you miss out even one, you are likely to encounter greater problems later on that are connected to the work that has come before. In other words, errors occurring in the basic work that are not put right, but instead are just taken on into advanced work, don't just disappear. They will resurface later to create real problems when it comes to the more difficult movements. If, for example, a horse finds it particularly difficult to execute a volte or flying changes on one rein, then it is more than likely that he wasn't ridden to be straight and even on both sides in his basic work. Finding the reasons for

these emerging problems isn't usually easy and is only really successful when the rider has understood what connects the elements of dressage training, in other words, the common thread linking them all together.

All of the exercises that are shown here can be done both in a manege or when out hacking. Young horses especially will find their own balance faster if they are worked on uneven ground. Schooling when out hacking is very effective but is rarely done by "purist" dressage riders due to reasons of time, a lack of hacking or even out of fear of the challenges that they may face when riding away from the safe confines of the school. The benefits far outweigh the disadvantages, however. The positive effect that riding out has on both horse and rider can considerably reduce communication problems that can waste both time and energy. At the start the experience of being ridden in an unknown environment can cause youngsters to be nervous or excited – a situation that makes it often easier for the rider to take charge and get the horse to pay more attention to him. The horse is more likely to listen so that the rider can work with lighter aids and achieve much more. In this way the horse learns to trust his rider in a more relaxed setting. In addition, uneven ground will cause the horse to have greater control of its body and to become sure-footed, as it will need to pay more attention to where it is putting its feet. By building a few of the dressage exercises into your ride, it will intensify the learning experience, increase the horse's motivation to learn and reinforce what has been learnt.

The work carried out when hacking is by no means a reduction in the level of the work, but on the contrary will cause a real jump in both learning and motivation on the part of the horse. Mutual trust, strengthened by riding out, is the prerequisite for the successful training of any partnership. The experience of doing something different and hacking out takes the rider away from the concept of "riding dressage" and of dominating the horse. However, *dressage means educating plus gymnastics whilst building mutual trust!*

Even if hacking out is preferable to training in a manege, school or arena (indoor or outdoor), all of these offer a multitude of possibilities for working your horse effectively. Leading the way are the individual dressage movements and schooling patterns and figures which make up a rider's toolbox. Due to their form and the sequence in which they are ridden, they literally help form the base on which the horse's training is built. At the start, relatively simple patterns on straight lines are used, such as going large, riding across the school to change the rein or riding down the centre line. They allow both horse and rider time and space to concentrate on such fundamental things as balance,

Even when out hacking dressage movements can be asked for and learnt. Photo: Tierfotografie Huber.

seat and the aids. Then curved lines, such as serpentines and circles of varying sizes, are added to the mix that demand the dressage basics to already be established. With the help of these tools the horse's gymnastic programme can be endlessly varied. Throughout a horse's entire dressage training career, the exercises and figures that are used should be varied in difficulty from easy to hard. The schooling figures that are repeated again and again become old friends. They give both horse and rider a certain degree of security since they are well known and accompany both, from the start, on their combined ways.

As a pace without impulsion particular attention has to be paid when riding the walk, so that no breaks in rhythm creep in. Photo: Tierfotografie Huber

Once rider and horse have found their centre of gravity then they will both be able to move together without hindering each other. The horse should hardly be able to notice its rider, since he won't interfere with his horse's balance. He, the rider, should be almost undetectable and in total harmony with every movement of his horse. With a well-balanced rider the horse can concentrate on new movements and on finding his own balance. Anyone who has ridden a three-year-old horse will confirm this experience. I can quite clearly recall a particularly good three-year-old novice that even after months of work on straight lines still swayed like a ship at sea. Since the gelding was so very obedient it was only something small that happened in the stable that sadly made me aware of its special quality – he was almost totally blind. The owner's only option was to find him a field where he could be safely kept and let him retire there to live out his life.

The work in the following chapters concentrates on allowing the horse to establish its rhythm, balance and suppleness on straight lines. The horse should be ridden flexed, but only gently bent through the turns. The most important pace when starting to train is the trot, since the rider is able to move in a regular two-beat rhythm without interfering with the horse's rhythm. Once the exercises can be successfully completed at a trot then you can move on to working in canter and walk. The walk, a pace of four beats, deserves our special attention. It is important to remain regular, with no breaks in rhythm, so be careful and never ride the walk, which is described as a pace without impulsion, with reins that are too short or with too much leg.

The balanced horse

A horse moving freely in the field has a certain natural balance that changes completely once it has a saddle and a rider's weight on its back. Through its dressage training, the horse has to find a new sense of balance between its forehand and hind quarters. For this reason, one of the basic lessons is working on the balance of horse and rider. The rider must learn to stay in balance on the horse's back in every situation, without tensing up.

Riding Diagonals

Riding diagonal lines across the school is one of the basic exercises involving horse and rider moving from one point on the school diagonally across to the other. These may either be long diagonals (corner markers F to H or M to K) or short diagonals (the corner markers to the centre markers E or B as appropriate). Even more advanced riders can use these exercises as a warm-up at the start of a training session but always starting with long diagonals. After warm-up, you can move onto the shorter diagonals, going from one of the corner markers to the centre markers or starting from E/B out to the corner marker across half of the school. Both serve to check whether the horse is on the rider's aids, in other words, whether the rider can close up and steer the horse using his leg, seat and reins.

Prerequisites

We begin this lesson once we have completed the phase of familiarisation of either the young horse or in case of an older one returning back to work but not much trained in dressage before. It is just as important that the horse understands the basic aids, such as leg pressure and the reins, and the rider can control its speed and direction.

Description of the exercise

Riding a diagonal is not just a matter of riding along a predetermined straight line, but instead it comprises a complicated sequence of events:

1. Riding through a corner before turning onto the diagonal, refer to page 34 as well,
2. turning onto the straight line,
3. riding an absolutely straight line,
4. arriving at the correct point on the track, just before the corner, and finally,
5. riding through the second corner.

> **Always maintain an even tempo and the same rhythm!**

To turn onto the diagonal the rider needs to sit up, look in the new direction and prepare for the turn with the inside leg gently pushing the horse forwards (known as a forwards-driving leg). Immediately after this, the rider should make the horse aware of the upcoming change in direction by lightly taking up and giving through the inside rein (more a squeeze and release of the hand). In the turn the inside rein is widened slightly and then brought back to the correct position. It is important that the horse's shoulder is turned in mainly through the rider's seat, with the rider

The rider's body helps to turn the horse's forehand in the new direction. Here the rider's inside hip could be turned in slightly more forward.

When turning onto the diagonal, don't forget to activate the horse's outside hind.

and, thus, the new turn, you will need to ensure that what now becomes your outside leg can help to prevent the horse from falling out. At the same time, the new inside leg encourages the inside hind to step forwards and underneath the horse. To turn back onto the track the rider sits into the saddle and again uses his seat as previously described. Finally, the corner should be ridden with an even contact on both reins.

Now we concentrate more on riding the diagonal line: the essential part when riding through the corner is that the rider sits securely in his centre of gravity, resulting in the same degree of suppleness and looseness in both horse and rider. The horse and its legs stay vertical, maintaining its balance and rhythm. Through the turn the same amount of weight is carried on each of the horse's four legs and the horse should find it easy to be ridden through the bend.

The rider maintains his central position in the saddle. The rider's hips, though, should be aligned with the horse's, slightly swinging inside forward and the shoulders should be parallel to the horse's shoulders. The rider's inside shoulder is moved slightly back to mirror the slightly turned-in seat, but always maintaining balance through the seat. As a result of moving the inside shoulder slightly back whilst sitting up, more weight will be put on the inside seat bone for a moment and the weight, although invisible to the observer, will be moved slightly to the inside. It is important, though, to remain sitting up straight! Stick your tummy out. The rider should always sit deep into the saddle and spread his weight evenly across both seat bones and the pubic bone (known as the three-point seat).

turning his seat to show the direction. This supports the horse's forehand turning off the outside track into the new direction of travel.

As soon as the turn has begun and the forehand has been turned through the seat, the rider needs to activate the horse's outside hind leg and steer the horse from a balanced seat straight along the diagonal. Here it is important to make sure that the line is precisely ridden. Before reaching the track

When riding through a corner, the inside hind leg should be encouraged to step through and under the horse.

When moving, the centre of gravity of horse and rider should remain the same. It is helpful if you think through what you are going to ride and use your seat to ask for the turn whilst containing the horse. The middle position is when you change from a driving to a turning leg aid!

tempo, as well as using a three-point seat to carefully turn the horse. The rider should always sit on this triangular seat.

When riding turns, always stay relaxed and enjoy the straight lines. Practice until you get it right, and then immediately take a break!

As soon as this series of movements has become a matter of routine for horse and rider, and the technical aspects of the movement have been mastered, then this exercise should be easy to do and require little energy. The rider will just need to give the signal for the horse to respond. Particular emphasis should be placed on rhythm and

How do you tell if your training is effective?
The horse will put more weight on the inside hind leg briefly in the turns and will step under the rider's centre of gravity. This will release its shoulder and allow it to turn more easily with an established rhythm. The contact to the rider's hand will become more secure. By repeating the turns

The diagonal should always be ridden dead straight. The rider here should shorten her reins and hold her hands up more.

onto the diagonal and ensuring a steady rhythm and regular tempo, the rider is able to improve a horse's looseness, balance and straightness.

Even with this relatively easy exercise you are still working on cementing, building and checking the mutual language of rider and horse: the aids. Since riding diagonals is not placing any great demands on the rider, this simple exercise offers the rider the opportunity to work on and improve the way that his seat, legs and hands work together. He is able to work on his balance, practice turning his seat into the turns and to pay particular attention to the independence of his hands which during the course of the turns should become stiller. The frequent repetition of riding diagonals in their many variations also demands the horse's concentration.

Problems and solutions

- The horse is rushing: sit quieter, control the rhythm, change the rein more often and ride in walk on a long rein.
- The horse is wobbling, i.e. not going straight: ride more forwards, rebalance your seat, keep your head up. Watch out that you don't collapse through your hips.
- The turn into the diagonal is too tight: give the inside rein quicker, position your inside hip more forward, use more inside leg and ride more forwards without rushing.
- The turn is too wide: engage the inside hind first, but contain more with the outside aids to contain the horse more between the aids.
- The quarters are falling out: outside leg more on the horse and contain the horse more with the seat and leg, ask for a slight lateral bend and sit quietly.

Variations

All of the diagonals are used to change the rein in a huge variety of possibilities. The horse can be ridden in a combination of the three basic paces.

- Repeatedly change the rein across the diagonal without actually going large. Ride the short side every time but always immediately change the rein. The rider has enough time on the diagonal to balance his seat and prepare for the next turn. The short side can also be ridden as a half circle without riding into the corners.
- Demand more by changing the rein on a short diagonal: after clearly turning the shoulder into the new direction of travel, the rider has less time due to the shorter distance to prepare for the next turn and also prepare his seat for the turn. It is important to really concentrate, even if this exercise seems to be easy!

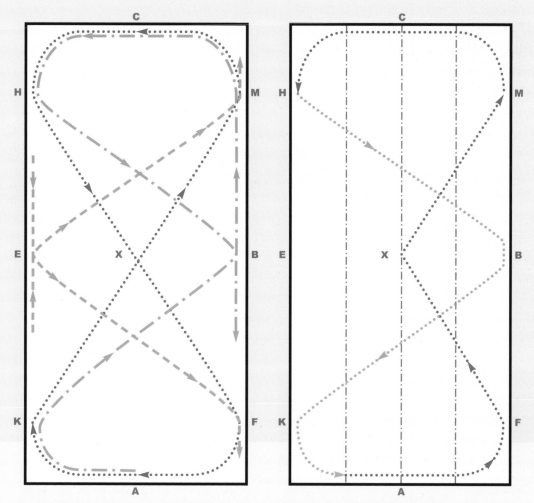

Blue line: diagonally changing the rein repeatedly.
Green line: repeatedly changing the rein on a short diagonal out of the corner.
Orange line: changing the rein on a short diagonal from E/B to the corners.

Blue line: zig zag serpentines involving sharp turns.
Orange line: changing the rein through the short diagonal twice in succession.

- Change the rein on the short diagonal but ride from E or B to the corner marker: whilst the first turn can be prepared in plenty of time the next turn looms quickly with a corner to quickly follow. The rider has a lot to do and needs to really concentrate.
- Zig zag serpentines: these are ridden from the corner marker to X and then back to the corner marker, paying careful attention to keeping to the required lines!
- Change through the short diagonal twice in succession: this requires a sharp turn of the forehand together with the quarters toward the centre point, and before getting there, a turn in the new direction. Ensure that you always ride forwards!

My tips for success

Young horses or horses being retrained can particularly gain in trust using these simple but effective exercises. It is worth repeating them daily at the start of a training session as often as necessary until the horse and rider are certain that they can communicate in a fraction of a second. Later, the riding of diagonals will be expanded by adding in more difficult movements, such as shoulder-fore, shoulder-in, travers or half pirouette, as well as medium trot or extended walk. Here, if not before, the rider will begin to use the aids individually. Leg, seat and hand are never all used at the same time, but rather after one another: first, the leg, then the rein. Using too many aids all at once demands too much of the horse and can cause him real stress.

Photo: Tierfotografie Huber

Riding lines off the track

Whilst riding on the track provides horse and rider with the comfort of being supported on one side, when riding lines away from the track (in German, literally, free lines), such as down the quarter line (5 metres off the track), the centre line or across the short diagonal, this support has to be dispensed with. The absence of any type of physical boundary or support dictates whether the line is free standing or not. It is important to ride these correctly – the horse needs to be ridden briskly forwards without rushing. This improves its balance so that in the corners, you don't get that "motorbike" feeling, as if the horse is tilting to the side.

Prerequisite

To carry out this exercise the rider needs to have a balanced seat. The horse needs to happily accept the aids and has found its rhythm.

Lesson description

In order to be able to ride an independent line, the rider needs to turn the horse off the track at the right moment. As usual, he starts the turn by asking with the inside leg and contains the horse's outside shoulder with the upper thigh. On a good contact through both reins, the horse should now turn in at a 90 degree angle onto the new line without the support of the outside of the track. After turning in, the outside leg on the girth acts to drive the horse forwards, keeping the horse straight. Keeping a good forward-going rhythmic pace makes it easier to ride a straight line. If

If the horse doesn't remain around the inside leg through the turns or it tends to lean over like a motorbike going around a corner, then you need to work to improve its balance.

Riding lines off the track helps to refine the aids and communication between horse and rider.

changing the rein, then the rider needs to flex his horse in the new direction about a horse's length before the track. Riding back onto the track in the new direction the rider turns his seat, changes the leg position, drives more forwards on the inside and holds with the outside leg and contains through both reins. The rider's weight should always stay centred on both seat bones and the pubic bone.

How do you tell if your training is effective?

Riding independent lines schools the rider's awareness of the inside and outside aids. The regularity of the horse's movement allows him to sit into the saddle better and gives him time to concentrate more on the horse. On the other hand, the horse learns to better understand the aids and to listen to its rider. The balance of both should clearly improve.

Problems and solutions

- The horse wobbles on the line: the rider needs to stay centred with his weight and seat and ride more forwards.
- The horse is rushing: keep the same rhythm in the turns and on the straight lines.
- The horse tries to return to the track: use more outside leg on the girth, ride briskly forwards and change the rein more often, making sure you repeat the exercise on both reins.

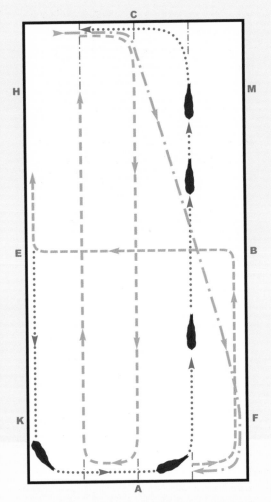

Orange line: alternate between riding the centre and the quarter line.
Green line: turn in at C or A and ride to the opposite corner marker.
Blue line: quarter lines
Yellow line: change the rein across the arena from between E and B.

Variations

- Change the rein across the middle of arena, ride down the centre line and change the rein and then ride across the middle again. The horse will concentrate more, and it will help to secure the rider's outside aids, together with the work into the corners, referring to page 34.

- Ride down the quarter line, across the arena on the E-B line and down the quarter line again: this involves riding lines off the track allowing the rider to check how well his aids are working whilst refining them.
- Centre line – quarter line: here, too, there is no opportunity for the horse to rely on the outside track for support allowing the rider to really work on the aids.
- Riding the diagonal from C or A to the corner point without changing the rein: the rider's outside aids need to contain the horse and the horse is ridden in a straight line to the corner point.

My tips for success

Riding free lines builds trust and shows the extent to which a horse is able to balance itself on a straight line. You should always practice this evenly both ways, frequently changing the rein. The balanced, centred seat and the rotated seat must be practised so that the horse is offered the right support and its balance isn't interfered with. This will help towards a faster understanding. Precisely this combination of free lines together with riding across the diagonal demands greater concentration from both horse and rider. Instead of just riding around and around on the outside track, the rider creates a varied combination in the warm-up phase. At the end of a session the use of this exercise serves to revise what has already been learnt and to relax the horse.

Remember: work on your seat and position every day.

Leg yielding

At the early stages of training, this exercise can be very useful for both horse and rider to get them both used to a new movement and the co-ordination of the variety of aids that are used. It teaches the rider to use the diagonal aids, with the inside leg working to push the horse into the outside rein which lightly catches the forwards movement. Due to this forwards-driving aid from the leg, the horse relaxes the jaw when flexed to the inside as it is being held through the outside hand.

Leg yielding involves a forwards-sideways movement with the legs moving diagonally across. The angle of movement from the starting point should be no more than 45 degrees. The rider sits relaxed in the saddle and uses his inside leg, positioned slightly behind the girth to ask the horse to step forwards and across the outside leg. The rider's outside leg supports and holds the horse from stepping too far round with the hind quarters. The forehand should lead so that the horse is being ridden in shoulder-fore (refer to page 83), and the rider's seat is turned slightly in the direction of the movement. This exercise is especially good for inexperienced riders who learn to use both the sideways-forwards and the holding aids. Here, too, all of the aids (seat, legs and hand) should never be given at the same time. The separate application of the aids demands that the rider learns to move each part of the body individually and independently from the other whilst staying relaxed. This exercise can be ridden in both walk and trot, but it is important, especially in walk to keep an even quiet tempo, moving each leg step by step and changing the rein often.

Sitting loosely and relaxed, the rider should feel each individual step made by the horse's hind legs through his seat. Working together like this, the horse should be able to move across without losing its balance. It will give the rider the feeling of having the horse in front of him, since it isn't falling back behind the aids.

Take your time: ask the horse to leg yield step by step, thinking of moving each leg individually. The horse should stay straight through the body with slight flexion.

My tips for success
It is important to be satisfied after only a few steps – less is more! For all this, though, the steps should be carefully and accurately ridden. Moving on to further training, leg yielding should give way to riding similar exercises on the circle (stepping across on the circle), shoulder-fore and shoulder-in. These exercises will serve to gymnasticise the horse a lot more as they involve more bend and more collection and so are more valuable for training.

The horse in bend

At some stage in a horse's training, a point will be reached when a horse that is ridden in straight lines, becomes a horse that is straight but that can bend. This is fundamentally important for the horse

Correct flexion and bend belong to a horse's basic schooling.

to be able to use its body in the best possible way when trying to improve the smoothness and suppleness in turns and circles. This will mean that the rider can follow the movements softly with his seat and the horse will be able to work through his back in an elastic and cadenced movement.

Square circles and circles

When working on a horse's bend, a range of proven and invaluable schooling figures are at your disposal. You should first of all concentrate on the all important circles, starting will the square circle. This figure, formed by riding from one circle point to the next as a square (see over) is the preliminary for riding proper circles. It is the starting point for increased suppling, ending with riding a round circle. The circle is a basic schooling figure on which the horse will be worked at every stage of its training up to Grand Prix and high school work. Working on a circle will help with longitudinal bend, when the horse bends through the length of its body. In reality, although this doesn't resemble a true anatomical representation of a horse, as a model it is very helpful to structure the rider's imagination.

Understanding and working through the individual steps in training might first of all appear to be a long process but is crowned with lasting success: the horse is schooled in small steps and must itself cooperate and follow your thoughts during the process. The horse won't be overtaxed, since each step taken on the "staircase" will be the same size, starting with the smallest and working towards the greatest of demands.

Prerequisites

Horse and rider will need to have found the right level of understanding, in which the aids – especially from the leg – are given correctly in a way in which the horse can clearly understand. The horse will go evenly and rhythmically in balance.

Lesson description

As mentioned in my introduction to this section, it is sensible to start with a square circle. To do this you will need to ride from each circle point to the next with four turns and four straight lines in between. Circle points divide a 20 metre circle into quarters, with one being at X, the second at A or C and the third and fourth 10 metres up each of the long sides from the end, midway between E/B on a 20 x 40 arena. The rider steers the horse through each of the turns as if he were riding a bike: he keeps the contact through both reins, allowing the outside hand though slightly forward to allow for a slight inward flexion. The rider should turn his seat through each of the turns, whilst at the same time driving more with the inside leg. This causes the inside hind leg to step more forwards and underneath the horse's centre of gravity and takes more of the weight through this leg. This causes the centre of gravity to shift slightly back. The rider's outside leg holds and supports the hind quarters during the turn so it doesn't lose its line. After each turn you need to ride briskly forwards towards the next point on the circle, using both legs to ride forwards. This helps to get the horse in front of the leg as well maintaining rhythm and impulsion. In summary, always ride well forwards, but don't rush!

The development of a well-ridden circle goes from the

1. "initial" steps on the circle through
2. "precise" riding on a square circle with increasing number of corners,
3. "improved" riding on the circle (riding in flexion) and, finally, then to riding of the
4. "perfect" circle; at this stage all movements can be ridden on the circle, from shoulder-in, turn on the quarters, counter canter and canter pirouette.

The corners of the "square" circle will get rounder as you work through this exercise (initially with fourcorners, then eight then 16), meaning that the horse's bend can also be intensified, stretching from the hind leg, through the back and the neck up to the rider's quietly held hands. You should think of the horse moving along the circle's line with its entire body, beginning from the tail, along the back vertebra by vertebra until reaching the head. When working on a circle both sides of the horse have to be suppled evenly with the muscles also being built up evenly. The rider should ensure, though, that the horse is worked a few more times

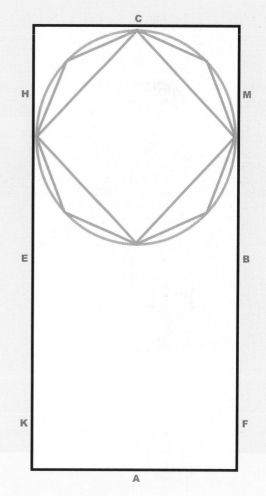

Orange line: *square circle*
Green line: *octagonal circle*
Yellow line: *circle*

on the rein that the horse finds more difficult on the circle. If the horse is hollow to the inside (appearing to bend more easily to this side) then you should forget about asking for more bend until the stiffer (outer) side has become more supple. On this rein, therefore, the horse should be evenly bent using just your seat and legs, keeping the neck as straight as possible. Don't be tempted to turn it using the reins! When the horse's hollow (or worse) side is to the outside, then the rider must maintain a firm contact with the outside rein. He

Basic work on the circle line is done to improve the lateral bending straightness

ters more. By doing this, the rider will really feel as if he is riding uphill and will not need to force the shoulder around in the turns.

> Don't use the reins to bend a horse, don't waste your energy! Think about it first!

How do you tell if your training is effective?

The initial work done on the circle serves to help to straighten the horse: its hind legs will follow in the tracks of the forelegs, stepping well under the horse's centre of gravity into an even contact through the reins. The bend through the length of the horse enables the rider's seat to feel the inside hind coming through, allowing the rider in turn to sit more deeply, as the horse literally pulls the rider down into the saddle.

Due to the hind legs' activity and the rounded back the horse is more contained and becomes more relaxed through the body and develops positive energy. Since the horse's centre of gravity moves more towards the quarters the forehand becomes lighter in the hand and allows the rider to ride turns more through his turned seat. The rider should maintain the rhythm at all times. More difficult circle work can be done by using the exercise which reduces and enlarges the circle's diameter.

Problems and solutions

If you are lucky enough to have mirrors, use these as a ballet dancer does to check what is happening with both you and your horse. Where are your legs? What is your seat doing? Where are your hands? Are you able to apply the aids individually and separately?

will also need to pay attention to controlling the outside hind leg, as well as ensuring that the rider's inside leg positioned on the girth can drive the horse forwards using the seat to control the movement. When circle work is done well the contact on both the stiff and hollow sides should become just as soft as training progresses and may even swap around during a training session. It is predetermined in the mother's womb which side of a horse becomes its stiffer side, and this is where the term "natural crookedness" comes from.

As the training of both horse and rider progresses, all turns should always be ridden using first the seat, then the legs and then the reins evenly. If the rider uses the seat and leg correctly through turns, avoiding the pulling around on the reins as if driving a carriage, then the trot and canter on the circle feel both rhythmical and full of purpose. Using correctly ridden turns will free up the horse's shoulder, since the centre of gravity will be moved back by activating the hindquar-

Usually, it is a rider's poor balance that interferes with his horse. If this is the case, then practice, practice, practice!

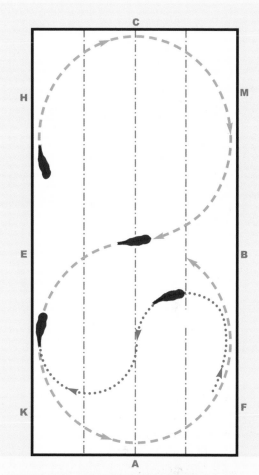

Orange line: *change of rein from circle to circle.*
Blue line: *changing the rein through the circle.*

- The horse turns more easily to one side than the other: always use the inside leg to drive the horse into the turn. On the more difficult rein support and restrict the horse with the outside rein, keeping a good contact throughout. Make sure that you have the same degree of contact through both reins, are sitting centrally and use your leg aids to keep the horse's attention.
- Falling out on the open side of the circle, possibly even turning around or falling out into the other circle: use more leg, knee and upper thigh, use the outside rein to clearly prevent the shoulder from falling out.
- The horse falls into the circle: use more inside leg and sit more centrally, maintaining your balance and keep the horse in front of the seat.
- The horse's forehand almost "sticks" to the track and is difficult to move off the track onto the circle line: make sure that you use the outside aids consistently and don't just start to use them as you reach the open side of the circle!
- The hindquarters are falling either to the outside or the inside: according to which it is, use the leg on the side that the horse is falling in or out to, to hold the horse and drive it forwards.

Variations

Circle work offers a multitude of variations and combinations of exercises:
- Changing the rein from one circle to the next over X: as you cross the middle line at X carefully turn your seat into the new direction of movement, ask the horse for the new bend and

don't forget to look in the new direction! The horse should stay in front of your seat. Over X make sure that you ride in a straight line for a horse's length. Ride this figure of eight exercise repeatedly. You will find that it becomes easier to flex the horse into the new bend, the turns will become smoother and the horse will become more supple and flexible.
- Change the rein through the circle: starting first in walk on a long rein, ask the horse to bend more, riding two half 10 metre circles to change the rein through the circle. It is very important

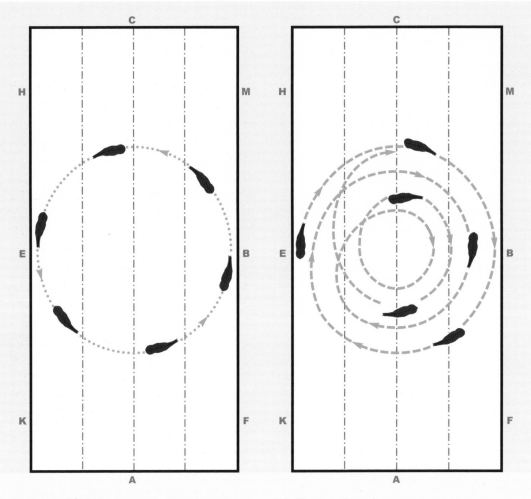

20 metre circle at E/B.   *Spiralling in on the circle.*

to pay attention to both the tempo and the rhythm throughout!

- Ride a 20 metre circle at E or B: with two open sides to this circle this exercise is more challenging! It is important to really pay attention to your outside aids, with your outside calf controlling the quarters and your knee and out side rein controlling the shoulder. The flow of the movement remains the same.
- Spiralling in and out on the circle as a loosening exercise: spiral in on an ever decreasing circle into the centre, then within a half circle

return out to the starting point. This exercise will help to create more bend through the horse's ribs. It is particularly important to pay careful attention to your leg aids to ensure that this exercise is done easily and well. Don't try to force this one, but repeat the exercise, which combines a high degree of longitudinal bend, alternating with asking the horse more forwards. Last but not least, remember that the tensing and relaxing of the muscles is important, since it is only relaxed muscles with good circulation that are built up quickly.

Pay particular attention that you use your seat to ask the horse to change the bend and minimise your use of the reins. Don't forget to always give your legs aids for the bend on one or both sides before you ask with your reins. If the horse doesn't "listen" to you, then it may well be that you are riding with too much hand. The rule of thumb is that you should push three times as much as you hold. If you hold less with your hand, then will also need to push less with your seat and legs.

Due to the constant turns, you will have every opportunity to practice the coordination of your aids and feel how your horse responds. You need to have refined the coordination of your aids to suit the horse you are riding. Really try to concentrate on what you are doing, as by doing this you will learn to feel what you and the horse are doing. The goal is to be able to feel what the hind legs are doing and where they are being placed with your eyes shut. Only then will you be able to feel what kind of influence your aids have on the horse. It will give you feedback as to whether the degree of intensity of your aids is correct or not.

A horse that is relaxed is more aware of its own body and, in particular, has a greater perception of its hind legs. The horse is easier to sit and will save both your energy as well as its own. The wonderful result of all of this circle work is a supple horse that works with you rhythmically and enjoys what it is doing, waiting in anticipation for what comes next. At the same time, muscles will be developed in the right places which in the short term will mean a clear improvement in the horse's top line.

An example of a horse that is swinging through its back with an active hind leg stepping through from behind. Photo: Tierfotografie Huber.

Riding Serpentines

As a result of the circle work, the horse is well prepared for the work on curved lines that follows. You have now reached a stage when you can begin to ask for greater bend through the horse (longitudinal bend), and serpentines are particularly good for this. Asking for an even and consistent bend on both reins is also important for the correct build up of muscles over the entire horse. In addition, serpentines have a positive effect on the horse's suppleness. The regular change of flexion and bend is one of the best ways to loosen the horse through the neck and poll. This loosening of the poll is an important component of achieving perfect "Losgelassenheit" (looseness, suppleness, relaxedness). The hindquarters will become easier to engage when the horse can be pushed through into a waiting and holding hand. This is the first stage in achieving submission or "throughness" (from the German Durchlässigkeit), which comes from the quarters over a swinging back into the bit.

Once the horse and rider find their mutual centre of gravity, the horse will gain more freedom through its shoulder.

Prerequisites

You should be able to ride straight lines and carry out the initial work on the circle without problems. The rider should be able to feel when the horse's hind legs leave the ground. Working on serpentines requires a secure three-point seat and the correct application of the aids.

Lesson description

Serpentines involve an uninterrupted change of bend from one rein to the other. At the start the horse is worked on both reins with a slight lateral bend which gets greater as work progresses. The rider needs to sit upright but must turn his seat in the direction of the bend whilst looking ahead at all times. When changing the rein and bend the horse needs to be ridden straight for one horse's

length so that the rider has time to turn in the new direction and change the horses bend. The rider's hand should be kept light.

After every change of bend the inside rein should be shortened slightly, which helps to secure the flexion through the poll. As soon as the horse is loose through the poll with a closed mouth gently chewing the bit, the rider can give with the rein. The rider then needs to use his inside leg to drive the horse diagonally out to his outside hand and controls the movement of the inside hind, moving forwards through the contact and his seat. The horse needs to always stay in front of your seat. The outside rein allows the bend, but controls it at the same time. The way the leg supports and drives the horse forward is exactly the same as with the work on the circle. The inside leg activates the hind quarters and the outside supports and holds it. The calf needs to close around the horse's sides.

Changing the rein frequently helps to secure both the rider's awareness and skill needed to change the bend and flexion of his horse. It also trains the rider in the use of diagonal aids: the inside leg driving the horse into the outside rein.

When changing the bend in serpentines maintain both the tempo and the rhythm!

1. Learn the effects of what you are doing.
2. Be aware: what should happen?
3. Practice the flow of the exercise and the aids.
4. Practice different variations: repeat often with variations
5. Make it automatic: do it without having to think about it so that the exercise can always be called upon!

How do you tell if your training is effective?

Due to the gymnastic value of this exercise and the frequent change of flexion through the poll, the rider will get a clear feeling of the horse swinging through its back and it will become more comfortable to sit. The horse will become more flexible and looser through its poll and the rider will find it easier to create the bend with no need for the hand to do more than maintain a light contact. Using this bending work on serpentines to change the rein will improve both the flexibility and the smoothness of the turns for both partners – horse and rider. This exercise is also the ideal preparation for lateral movements.

Serpentines are also very useful as they also train the rider's seat to follow the movement of the horse, turning with the horse as the direction changes. A rider needs to practice this until it becomes automatic, refining the aids so that the horse learns to follow them obediently. The more the combined centre of gravity frees up the horse's shoulder, the better a horse's paces will appear and the more balanced they will become.

Problems and solutions

• The horse wobbles on the line and doesn't go straight: maintain the balance and use your aids to support the horse and sit straight.

• The quarters fall out: use your outside leg to prevent the quarters falling out or drive more strongly forwards. You need to focus the horse's attention on you.

• The forehand turns too quickly – a bit like a motorbike round a corner: use less hand, hold more with the inside leg and once again make certain you are sitting in balance with the horse.

• Losing rhythm in the turns: go back to working on the circle to regulate rhythm and tempo and check what you are doing with your hands.

• The horse is tilting its head: allow the flexion through the outside rein but maintain the contact on both reins, pushing the horse up into your hands.

• No flexion: at halt ask the horse onto the contact and flex gently to both sides. Use all of your aids together to create energy from behind but maintain the contact at halt until the horse gives through the poll with its mouth still closed – think of a piping bag filled with icing – create a constant pressure without anything actually coming out.

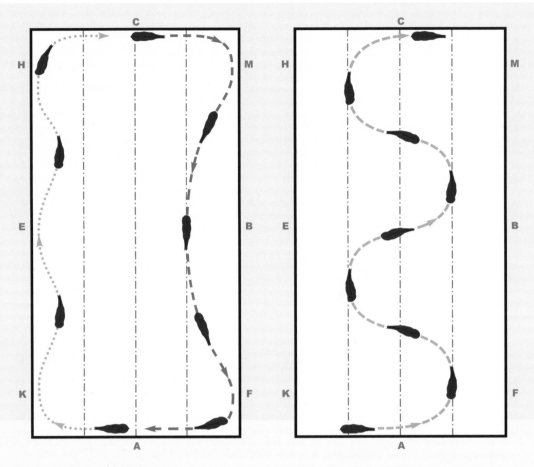

Blue line: a simple one loop serpentine.
Orange line: two loop serpentine.

Serpentine along the centre line.

- The horse goes on the forehand, leaning on your hands: lift your hands and hold them up, asking for the turns with a softer hand.

Variations

Serpentines offer countless possibilities for variations:

- Ride a simple one loop on the long side: requires two changes of flexion.
- Ride two loops on the long side: requires four changes of flexion.
- Serpentine down the centre line. Make certain the loops are even and rounded but only ride

only as far as the five metre line on each side. Careful attention needs to be paid to the aids given through the leg and the reins.
- Full serpentine going across the full width of the arena, with three to six loops, in canter with transitions through walk or trot: this is very effective for working on suppleness, bend, through ness and the start of collection. The chance to ask for and achieve everything in one exercise!
- Ride half a serpentine to the five metre line, then riding a ten metre loop in the form of a ten metre circle over the centre line: this demands good bend, balance and flexibility. Make sure that

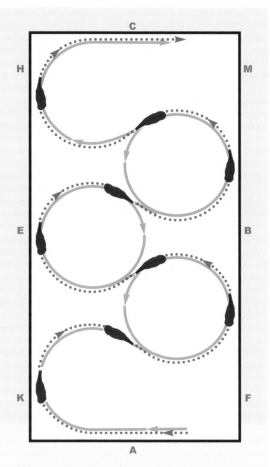

Blue line: *S-shaped serpentine.*
Orange line: *Serpentine with voltes.*

Using this set of exercises you will be able to improve the horse's ability to bend, its "throughness" (Durchlässigkeit) and notice an improvement in the activity of the quarters on a daily basis. It will also have a straightening effect, due to the even suppling of the horse on both reins. In the serpentines it is especially important that the rider's hands are equally soft on both reins, even on the stiffer side consistently give through the rein. The horse mustn't lean on the hand, but rather seek a soft contact. The straightening work should always be ridden in a good rhythmical forwards tempo.

I regard this work on the horse's bend utilising serpentines as incredibly valuable to achieving an optimal degree of suppleness with a horse at as early as stage in its training as possible, without wasting energy. Using targeted work such as this the horse is then prepared to move on to further training. Later, you will be able to build into the serpentine work voltes, transitions, flying changes or even piaffe work. It focuses the horse's attention and increases its flexibility, whilst allowing you to be creative in developing variations which can cover a range of the training areas on which you are placing emphasis and working.

the impulsion is maintained throughout the bends.
- Serpentine with integrated voltes: increases the difficulty in all areas. Pay attention that you stay on the correct line!
- Three loop serpentine in canter with no change of leg, moving for true (smaller serpentine) to counter canter (bigger serpentine). This improves balance considerably.
- Out of a three loop serpentine ride a half circle from the corner markers in counter canter back to the long side: this demands a greater degree of bend and requires the horse to step more through from behind.

Now the work becomes even more interesting and asks even more of the more experienced rider.
Carry on!

A corner of the arena isn't just the end of the long side but is an important exercise that can improve a horse's suppleness.

Riding through the corners

At first, riding corners may not appear to be a particularly demanding exercise, since they appear automatically at the end of each long side. You have to ride around the corner since not to do so would mean you would run into the sides of the arena! For me, the riding of these corners is very useful to work on to feel whether the rider is cor-

rectly turning his seat and whether the horse is bending correctly through the turn. Riding the corners correctly is good preparation for many of the lessons to follow, including the lateral work. The corner must be ridden using the correct aids: driving the horse forwards into the corner, half halt, bend, sit correctly, and then forwards out of a quarter circle into the next exercise.

This challenges both the horse's concentration and readiness to collect, – in other words, the degree to which the forehand and quarters are in balance. The balance should be on a ratio of 1:3.

To ride completely around the arena involves riding four corners; when you include a change of rein then it is six corners. Use each turn carefully and you will see enormous progress in a short time in the horse's training.

Prerequisites
Before the corner, you should check that the horse is in rhythm and that the horse is on the aids. Depending on the level at which the horse has been trained, it should have the correct degree of bend through its body and have experience of working on the circle. When warming up, the corners can be rounded off before being incorporated into the training as a proper exercise and ridden consciously with correct rhythm and impulsion. I can recall a young gelding that due to its big movement couldn't be ridden deep into the corners. Only when we came to the collected work I could really ride the corners on him well. Even to this day if he isn't working through from behind correctly, it is still difficult to ride him through the corner and go sitting on him in trot.

Lesson description
The level of training will determine how deep a corner is ridden. Every rider should be aware of the suppling effect that this exercise has on a

horse. The young horse, as well as the older, stiffer one, can cut the corner as much as is required until the bend is gradually improved without loss of rhythm. Even at the start of training, however, the corner should be correctly utilised.

Using a half halt, the rider prepares the horse for the corner and uses his inside leg more to push the inside hind leg more forwards. The outside leg, positioned just behind the girth, holds the horse and ensures that it stays on the correct line without drifting out. The rider sits in balance, turning his seat into the bend while his outside hand allows the flexion and bend, and the inside hand asks for the correct flexion. Carry your hands forwards, maintaining a soft contact. The horse's quarters should follow the forehand through the corner, stepping more through from behind.

Riding out of the corner, the rider's outside leg should come forward slightly, asking the outside hind to step more forward. Changing the rein frequently will ensure that the horse bends "through" its ribs around the rider's inside leg. This will mean that the horse will show no tension in the inside bend. Between the corners ride forwards, ensuring the horse is straight so that there is alternation between bending and then riding forwards.

Another useful exercising is to double the effect of the corner. Here, the horse is ridden straight into a corner with the rider then immediately using the inside leg strongly on the girth to turn the quarters so the horse's quarters literally almost "skid" round the corner. This reaction is provoked from the inside hind, the idea of which is to get the horse to respond to a finer aid and get its attention quicker. It will learn to respect the aids from the leg more and respond faster to them, enabling the rider to use finer aids. The forehand is turned more sharply in the new direction and the outside leg is used to push the horse forwards out of the corner.

Always ride forwards through the corner and maintain the movement. Concentrate on sitting up straight in the centre of the saddle in a three-point seat.

How do you tell if your training is effective?

If the corner is ridden correctly then it should be easy to ride the horse through the corner off your seat, creating energy for the next exercise. Always assuming that the horse has been trained to respond correctly to the rider's aids, the horse should be using its body more intensely in the corner for a brief moment in order to bend and take more weight through its inside hind. All of this

After a corner a horse should become more forwards-going. Corners help to train the horse's entire body.

careful preparation up until now will be invaluable to the work that follows, such as riding extended paces out of the corner, half circle and back to the track, turning down the centre line, shoulder-in or half passes. Corners will help loosen up a horse, will make them more sensitive, come more through, will help collection and self-carriage, while training the horse's entire body. Out of the corner comes a horse that is more motivated, going more forwards with greater freedom through the shoulder!

Problems and solutions

- The horse rushes: go back onto a circle and work on rhythm.
- The horse gets slower: keep the horse in front of the leg, maintain impulsion by not riding quite so deep into the corner.
- Falling out through the shoulder or the quarters: use your aids to contain the horse, checking that you are applying your aids correctly.
- The horse is tilting its head: allow the outside hand forwards and then hold.
- The horse leans on your hands: use less leg, don't hold as much through the reins and ask for less bend to get the horse more used to taking the weight through its quarters.
- The horse has trouble bending on one side: go back to working on serpentines and circles.
- The horse is over bent with a short neck: use less hand, drive more forwards and round off the corner slightly.

Special problems

A corner is and remains a corner, so there are no opportunities for variation here. So, at this stage instead I would like to highlight issues that might occur when turning off the outside track onto other lines other than in the corner and how to deal with them:

- When turning up the centre line or in at B or E, always pay particular attention to the outside hind and use your outside hand to help the relieved fore-hand turn.
- Use short and light inside half halts to ask for the bend. As soon as the horse has turned in, straighten the horse and ride forwards.
- The same applies when turning after the corners onto the long diagonals which have to be ridden more carefully and longer, this movement equating to a three quarter circle. Maintain your balance throughout and always keep the horse in front of the leg.

My tips for success

For me, a correctly ridden corner acts as a touchstone, an important test in the training of a horse. It shows me whether both horse and rider can maintain rhythm, suppleness, bend and carriage. It is only possible to ride a corner well off the outside leg when the horse doesn't rush away from the inside leg but instead maintains the energy created in the movement. This leads to the horse showing more expression and cadence. Horse and rider begin to truly "dance".

Engage the quarters, create energy within the horse without getting faster and don't override!

In this body-building programme never neglect a corner! Ride every corner carefully and with attention so that before every next exercise and

A horse moving rhythmically and in cadence will start to "dance". The horse's movement will become much more expressive.

for the preparation of later ones you can really enjoy the improved freedom through the shoulder and self-carriage that it creates. A corner is good training for the horse's entire body, since it helps to tighten the stomach muscles and relaxes the back. The rider's calf should remain consistently against the horse's sides, driving forwards to create energy and not speed.

Successful training for me means that your horse will remain fit and healthy for longer and will be able to have potentially a longer competitive career. In addition, you will belong to the group of riders that put less miles on the clock and will reach their goal sooner without wearing their horse out. Remember to always take breaks when training so that you don't overload your horse's ability to concentrate. Save you and your horse's energy for the more difficult lessons later!

Don't forget to give you and your horse plenty of breaks when training. It is time to stop when things are going well!

The volte and its variations

A volte is a circle with a diameter of 6 - 10 metres; from the point of view of riding them, though, they consist of several corners stuck together. They can be ridden in walk, trot and canter. Voltes can greatly help to improve a horse's suppleness and bend. The smaller the volte, the greater the gymnastic effect on the horse and the more collection is required. The rider has to sit carefully and needs to concentrate on how the aids are

Riding a volte, here in canter, should be carefully prepared, since there is little time to correct mistakes.

applied. Riding voltes isn't old fashioned, especially not at a time when dressage is getting increasingly technical in nature.

We should be aiming to use voltes to more effectively train our horses. To keep our partnership as horse and rider going for longer it should be our goal to ensure that our horse is supple and gymnastically exercised. For this reason, using voltes and their variations, such as figures of eight, is a sensible way to train!

Prerequisites

To ride a volte you need to know how to ride out of a corner correctly. The horse should bend evenly on both reins and thanks to the correct work already done on the circle is supple and straight. The rider needs to ride through a seat

that turns in the direction of the movement without losing his balance and so offers the horse support. The rider needs to move in harmony swinging with the horse's back to avoid interfering with the horse's movement during the volte.

Lesson description

When riding a volte it is just as important as with the work on the circle that you create an even bend. Here, too, you should start by thinking of riding a volte consisting of four individual corners, which is easier for a rider to imagine. If this can be done well, then we move the training on by riding two half voltes. The rider has less time than with a larger circle to get the correct bend on a circle with such a small diameter. The second half of the volte will tend to get larger but the rider's leg aids should keep the horse on the correct line. It is noticeably harder to maintain suppleness of movement on a smaller volte. At the start it is alright to ride a slightly larger volte (eleven metres) but make sure that the second half is kept round and think of riding four even quarters – i.e. four corners.

Include 10 metre voltes in your training programme for a few weeks. If this goes well, then start to build in smaller voltes. Due to the smaller diameter the horse's impulsion and your aids have to be spot on: prepare the horse by using half halts, make sure it is truly off your aids and moving through from behind so that it gives through the poll. By doing this, it will be easier to ride the volte and the horse is better prepared to accept the aids.

During the volte itself there is no time to improve on impulsion since the rider will be busy ensuring that the volte is ridden as a circle. If the volte becomes too small then the inside leg will be used more and if too big, it is the outside leg that is used more.

The quarters will be engaged so that they step through underneath the horse and the horse will appear to move "uphill". To achieve this, the rider's outside leg contains and holds the hind leg. The inside hind will be encouraged to step more underneath the horse with the rider's inside leg. If the hind legs can be engaged then the front and back legs will move in line on the same track. The withers will lift up and, with a greater degree of freedom through the shoulder, the horse will appear to move uphill.

The shoulder is permanently turned and held with the outside leg so that it moves precisely on the line of the volte. The rider's seat that is both quiet and turned in the direction of the bend gives the horse a degree of security so that the exercise can be repeated or changed at any stage. It always needs to be ridden in balance so that all four legs of the horse can carry its own body and the rider in its centre of gravity so that you never get that feeling of a motorbike going around a corner. This is crucial so that the horse can be turned through the rider's seat. When the rider and horse find this exercise easy then you have almost reached perfection!

At this stage the horse will be ready to allow itself to be ridden off the rider's seat. The contact should be elastic and not fixed. The rider should have an even contact through both reins and the horse will be swinging through its back into to the contact without falling out through the quarters. Front legs and hind quarters are linked like a bridge. The neck will be bent according to the angle of the bend through the horse's body, and never more.

The rider rides rhythmically and controls every stride without the horse beginning to rush. If the volte is ridden correctly, then the horse will move supply and smoothly throughout without losing impulsion. The rider will be carried with

The volte is the basis for all lateral movements.

the movement, containing the horse with a quiet leg.

How do you tell if your training is effective?
Voltes prepare for lateral work. The increased bend has a positive effect on:
• giving through the inside rein,
• establishing rhythm
• suppleness
• the elasticity of the paces
• straightness with impulsion
• improving the horse's ability to carry itself and its rider

During this work, which involves increased bend, the ability of the back to swing through and the cadence in the trot will be improved. In canter the movement will become more expressive and contained. Riding voltes in canter – true and counter canter – is an important training tool that

No ambitious rider can afford not to use a qualified instructor. Photo: Tierfotografie Huber

experiencing this for the first time will recognise what we mean. When riding such a small circle the impulsion that has been created shows itself in real cadence, meaning the rider can collect the horse without having to pull on the reins and really feel the horse's quarters come up underneath him.

> When lengthening steps and strides, only create as much energy as you can hold and can use.

Problems and solutions

As with any exercises involving turns, here, too, there are a multitude of problems that can occur. Even if you can only solve one each day, you will get closer to achieving a real feel for riding.

helps to improve the horse's ability to carry itself and to improve its straightness.

> To better check how you are progressing, having someone film you can be useful, as can taking lessons with a qualified riding instructor.

> The energy in the horse's movement must be created before the volte. Only then will the horse stay in front of the rider's seat throughout the volte.

Due to the shifting centre of gravity and the improved elasticity of its movement and paces, the horse is ideally prepared for the lateral movements.

A further effect that can be felt is when impulsion is maintained through the volte. Every rider

- The horse is losing its balance: use your hands more evenly, sit straight, drive forwards and use both of your legs to hold the horse's hind legs on the line of the volte.
- The volte isn't round: check whether the horse is moving through from behind straight, go back to the circle and work on the longitudinal bend!
- The hind quarters are falling out: check the bend, use more outside leg and rein.

- Irregular rhythm: give more through the hands, go large and work on serpentines as well as circles.
- The horse is rushing: cause is likely to be that the horse is too much on the forehand. Check whether the horse can be ridden through a corner and stay in rhythm without leaning on the forehand. If it can't, go back and do more work on the circle.

Variations
- Ride voltes in the corners and at B or E supported by the outside track.
- Ride voltes on the centre line at walk, trot and canter or at A or C without returning to the outside.
- Volte – single or double loop along the long side – volte. Combine voltes with other types of serpentines (four, five or six loops). This

Voltes in the corner and at B.   *Voltes combined with a single loop on the long side.*

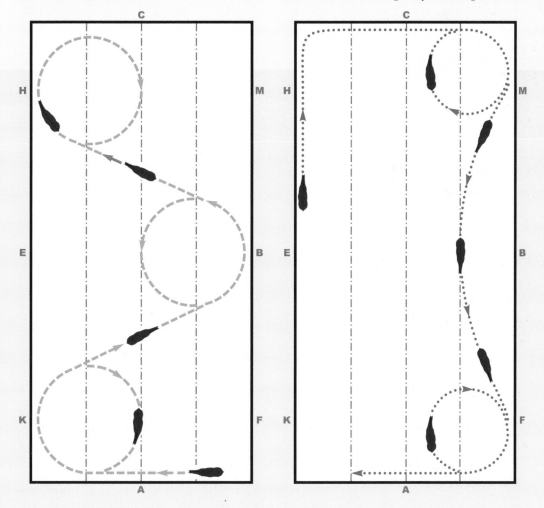

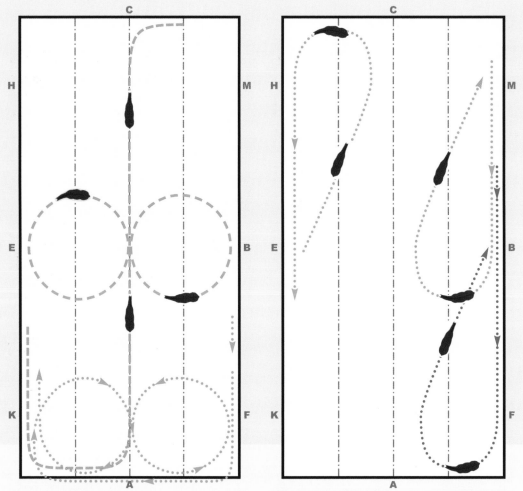

Figure of eight voltes.
Green line: on the centre line.
Orange line: off the outside track.

Blue line: half volte out of the corner to change the rein.
Green line: the opposite, riding into the corner in a half volte to change the rein.
Orange line: half volte at B.

shows clear bend on both reins in one exercise.

- Figure of eight using 10 metre voltes ridden on the short side or at X, or down the centre line or from E to B or B to E. This helps flexion and loosens the poll.
- Volte with change of rein after a half volte, out of the corner or into the corner. This will get and keep the horse's attention.

- Integrate two or four voltes into a larger circle: This demands more bend on smaller and larger circles.
- Spiral in on a circle until you reach a volte, transition to walk or ride shoulder-fore back out and then ask for some extension: this combines bend and collection with creating movement off the leg.

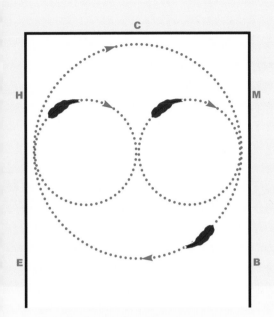

Integrate voltes into the circle.

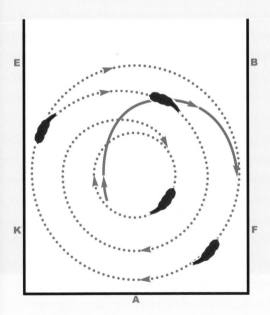

Spiral in on the circle.

Use the gymnastic effect of voltes as a way of checking the consistency of the bend and to improve suppleness.

My tips for success

If you think that voltes are an unnecessary evil then this isn't the right book for you. If this is the case, then I can only recommend that you look for a different book on how to ride dressage correctly. In my training programme, riding voltes is one of the exercises that is central to a rider's skills advancing. It is important to use voltes to perfect the horse's longitudinal bend and the ability of the quarters to carry it.

All of the harder exercises that develop out of this work will follow in a natural progression. My rule is always to work from the easier to the harder! Shut your eyes and feel!

If you have followed the training given in the previous chapters and built the work using voltes into your training plan, then you have trained honestly and will be able to enjoy your success. It is important to go back and check this work daily: it is like learning a new language or learning to play the piano. The skill and success gained in riding smaller voltes with ease and the required improvement in the horse's ability to carry itself will clearly show you whether you are on the right track and can start the more difficult work.

Allowing the horse to stretch down into the contact is an exercise that makes it clear whether the rider is riding correctly off her seat. Here, the lower leg should be more on the girth.

Allowing the horse to stretch and take the contact down

When you ask a horse to stretch and take the rein down you are asking the horse to stretch over its back gradually in the direction of the rider's hand whilst staying in balance, and this exercise can be done at any pace. This exercise is fortunately still ridden in tests as "free walk on a long rein". In the German equivalent, the term specifies that the horse must "chew" the reins out of the rider's hands. It is ideal for checking both the horse's suppleness and the rhythm during daily training sessions, as well as to see where the horse is in its training and to allow it to relax.

Even in the more advanced movements this exercise plays an important role. By means of this exercise every rider, whether beginner or professional, should check his horse's suppleness and relaxedness (Losgelassenheit) or its self-carriage by giving and retaking the reins. At any stage of an exercise it should be possible to allow the horse

to stretch and take the reins down: whether this is immediately after a canter, walk transition or during a pirouette. If it is possible, the rider has been successful in riding the horse from his seat and the hands will almost become superfluous. It is important that the engagement through the quarters is maintained and the horse stays together on the aids, whether being ridden on a long or short rein.

Prerequisites
The horse will have progressed through the initial phase and responds well to the rider's aids. It will have found its rhythm and will be showing the beginnings of true suppleness stepping through correctly from behind. Thanks to this it will be able to maintain its balance even without a contact through the reins.

Description of the exercise
Allowing the horse to stretch and take the contact down can be ridden in walk, trot and canter. To prepare for it the rider needs to check his seat and using half halts check the balance between the forehand and hind quarters. The hand then needs to allow forwards slightly and then be held in position. The rein should be gradually taken down whilst maintaining the contact. It is important to continue driving the horse forwards with your calves flat on the horse's sides. It helps to imagine that the horse is "sucking" your legs against its belly. Driving the horse evenly into the hand with the horse's neck stretched out and a relaxed back will give the horse the necessary confidence to continue to work in a relaxed way. The gradual lengthening of the horse's outline into a stable but not fixed contact continues until the reins are at full length. It should be possible for the rider to take up the reins again at any stage, whilst maintaining the same rhythm and tempo.

Using a passive seat the rider should tighten his upper stomach muscles – it is helpful to think of pushing your stomach out forwards. He should sit relaxed but straight in the centre of gravity, following the movement through the pelvis. This will also help the horse's back to swing with the movement as well.

Whether the reins are short or long, the contact between the rider's hand and the horse's mouth should be carefully co-ordinated, remaining elastic and even on both sides.

How do you tell if your training is effective?

The stretched outline with the appropriate degree of tension through the body is precisely the purpose and the result of this exercise. The rider can check that his seat is independent from his hands and by giving the hands forwards the horse is moving freely. He should be able to ride on a long rein without any problems, utilising the combined centre of gravity. He will feel the hind legs swinging through and under the horse, the relaxed and supple back and the horse's rhythm.

This exercise can be repeated again and again from a passive seat working on using increasingly finer aids. The stomach muscles act as a counter balance to the horse's back and neck that when tightened slightly relieves the back. The stretching of the horse's body, combined with a positive tensing of the muscles due to correctly ridden exercises, is crucial for a correct training in dressage. Only this stimulates good circulation around the muscles and limbs and there will be no problems with over oxygenation or sore muscles. Using this basic training programme, horses will be able to perform to a high level without straining themselves, just like human athletes, and without getting fed up. In addition, the horse will remain mentally happy, will be keen to learn and be prepared for more muscular body-building.

Try to feel the physical tension that exists through the horse's body when stretching down. Get down on all fours and feel this positive tension in your own body.

Problems and solutions

The horse will only be able to stretch and take the reins down when rhythm and suppleness are guaranteed. A rider with a poor seat will have problems completing this exercise. The following problems may occur:

- The rider's hand is too high, which encourages the horse to either fall behind the rein or to lean on the hand: drop your hands, breathe out and clearly ask the horse to move forwards.
- The hand is too fixed, causing resistance through the horse's mouth and back: keep your arms loose, allow the hands to drop and start the exercise with longer reins.
- In giving too quickly you lose the contact and the horse comes off the aids: keep a flexible contact through the reins combined with continuing to drive forwards. Make sure that you keep a supple seat.
- You lose the contact: go back to working on curved lines, continuing to drive evenly forwards in measured doses and allowing only a few centimetres at a time but alternating with riding forwards.

A horse will only understand your aids when given from a straight and correct seat.

- Sitting crooked, the horse loses its balance and tips over: work on your seat at walk, riding towards a mirror to better assess your seat–imagine the girth is very loose!
- You sit too heavily in the saddle causing the horse to rush and hollow its back and neck: sit upright and give the hand forwards, riding quietly on and possibly transitioning down. Repeat this several times.
- The horse is falling out: maintain impulsion, riding trot-canter transition forwards, without forcing them. This improves the balance point between the hind quarters and the forehand.

Variations

On both curved and straight lines ask your horse to stretch and take the contact down:

- At walk: concentrate on stretching, contact and an even four-beat walk.
- In trot: ask for a good forwards tempo without rushing, a good contact and an open seat with a relaxed back, keeping your balance.
- In canter: you should be looking for a supple response to the aids, a well bent and flexed horse with an uphill outline and a stretched neck and back. Sit up and don't tip forwards.
- Ride over Cavaletti: this will increase stretching and the horse will use its stomach muscles more. The horse's nose should be on a level with height of the point of the shoulders.
- At a gallop: ride the horse from a forward seat with a loose rounded back with active quarters without rushing. The horse should be on a light but deep contact and the mouth should be in line with the point of the shoulder.
- Ride uphill in all paces: the horse should stretch and take up a good contact. This is excellent training for the back with as little as ten minutes of riding uphill offering real benefits. Ride downhill only at a quiet walk.

- Uneven contact or incorrect flexion: work more on straightness by changing over to circles and serpentines.
- The horse's back is tight: drive the horse forwards less, since more pushing doesn't necessarily mean more success! Use half halts to introduce the exercise.
- The horse is not moving through enough from behind: keep your leg on, ask clearly and rhythmically for the quarters to come through in time and not against the rhythm. Maintain the balance between the forehand and the hind quarters.

Riding in a forward-going canter offers variation in a training programme.

My tips for success

Only a rider that has an independent seat and rides in an effective and relaxed way is capable of training his horse to be supple and relaxed. It is for this reason that student riders at the Spanish Riding School in Vienna train for so many years on the lunge. Even when training at home it is helpful if you can be lunged so that you can concentrate on your seat and on achieving the optimal combination of the aids applied correctly, to ensure that horse and rider understand the other.

Horse and rider should be able to complete this exercise in walk, trot and canter without difficulty. If they can then they are on the right training path.

Allowing the horse to stretch and take the contact down creates a happy and relaxed horse that is capable of carrying out harder exercises. Even as a stretching and relaxing break between collected work this exercise will prove to be very useful. This switching between relaxation and tension, both physically and mentally, is common with other sports and will significantly increase the performance potential, since its loosened muscles are always being adequately supplied with oxygen. The oxygenation of the muscles is significant for their healthy development. Every human athlete will carry out a thorough warm-up, whether a swimmer, skier or sprinter. Why then shouldn't we use this knowledge daily with our horses. You train your horse so you need to keep it healthy and fit.

Working towards proper collection

Following the work on the basics, which involves loosening and balancing the horse, and getting it to respond sensitively to the aids, we can now begin to ask more of the horse's hind quarters. The hind quarters, which are one of the most powerful parts of the horse, should carry a greater load in order to relieve the forehand and prevent the horse from overtaxing.

Going actively into collection

The hind quarters are responsible for most of a horse's power. They are the horse's motor and responsible for providing its energy and carrying power. The flexion of the haunches is important for taking up the load with the hind legs pushing off when moving forwards. The hind legs should step forwards with purpose, carrying the energy from the back to the front almost as if the horse were dancing.

Upwards transitions into trot and canter

This apparently easy exercise conceals many facets within it. It is all about keeping the entire horse's body supple and active whilst as little energy as necessary. This can be done by riding transitions from a slower into a faster pace. It is like an easy and simple fitness programme.

The hind quarters are a horse's motor, to be kept active and motivated.

Prerequisites

Working through the back is indispensable for correctly ridden transitions. The looser the horse's back is the better the rider's aid can be communicated. On the other hand, though, the rider needs to have a relaxed, balanced seat so that he doesn't interfere with the horse.

An interesting case to look at is that of a 13-year-old black gelding, that came to me as a trained horse. At the start I was barely able to ride this horse using normal aids. Whatever I tried in the way of driving aids had no effect whatsoever. Every day turned in to a battle of strength that wasn't any fun for either of us. It wasn't just hard

work for me, but the gelding tired quickly as well. I had to rethink my approach and took off my spurs. From then on, the horse that was already "trained" to medium/advanced level started a new phase in his career as he couldn't revert to any of his previous patterns of behaviour. My goal was to reach him by exerting as little effort as necessary and it worked: the gelding understood very quickly that he had to use his hind legs first of all to then be able push himself up into trot and canter. He had learned to run again. To this day, the horse's entire body owes its new shape to this work. Not only has his top line considerably improved, but you can also see that he has a totally different attitude to his work, being more motivated and willing. Today he radiates a contented and relaxed attitude with which he completes all of his movements up to piaffe and pirouette happily and with ease.

Description of the exercise

The rider needs to prepare himself to ask for the next pace and really think about the new rhythm in his head: four-beat at walk, two-beat at trot and three-beat to canter. It is important that the horse is kept straight by keeping the forehand in line with the quarters. When moving off or changing up into the next pace, the horse needs to be put on the aids and be brought into a state of positive physical tension. To do this, the rider needs to sit up consciously, breathe in whilst asking with the leg positioned on the girth for the new rhythm. All of these signals serve to bring the hind legs forward and engage the horse's motor. You should think of riding the hind legs first and a moment later the forehand. To move off, the carefully applied leg on the girth acts to prepare the horse to then move forwards. This serves to engage the hind legs to move forwards at the required moment, ensuring that the horse doesn't get faster and its body is held together during the move off. It should remain on the rider's aids and will actually get shorter through the body.

Before cantering you need to use a half halt to get the horse's attention. It will take up its weight through its inside hind and should lighten through the hand. This is exactly the moment to ask for canter! The horse's whole body will be put to work when the rider gives the signal by driving the active hind leg underneath a relaxed back up into the rider's hand. The stomach muscles, the hind legs and the neck held in self-carriage will all get stronger through

Success without force: a resistant gelding has become an impressive dressage horse. Photo: Blacky

repetition. We are continuously forming our horses into almost a "work of art", meaning that muscles are built up in the right place. When the hind quarters are engaged the rider will get an uphill feeling through the horse's entire body and is easy to sit.

The horse takes the rider with him through the movement and follows the aids given off the rider's legs. It stays in front of the seat. The upwards transitions become easy and don't cause any problems. A correct transition is recognised by its quietness. It can be done anywhere and everywhere across all paces.

How do you tell if your training is effective?

Before moving off and before an upwards transition the horse is metaphorically speaking "in the starting gates". It is important that the energy created remains inside the horse! It should obey the rider and his aids willingly and be an easy ride. When relaxed through its back the horse will create real impulsion out of the quarters and the hocks, enabling it to step well under its centre of gravity and come up through the shoulder. The first walk, trot or canter stride is easy to see and will be carried out with a clear uphill tendency and contracted stomach muscles. The horse rounds up, coming through from behind and creates a feeling of positive tension. This means that the back rounds up and the hind legs come through underneath the rider. This increases the sensitivity of the now shorter framed horse that is ready to work, with active quarters and improved impulsion that can successfully carry out the transitions.

Transitions are a daily necessity in all types of riding and improve the suppleness of the horse's entire body, as well as its acceptance of the aids.

An example of a horse showing a lovely uphill canter: wonderful and with plenty of freedom through the shoulder.

Problems and solutions

- Resistance when moving off or with upwards transitions: check where your leg is and get the horse's attention before asking for the move off. Wake it up by tapping your leg once more strongly behind the girth. If the horse reacts by going forwards praise him and ride on with the normal strength of aid.
- The horse lifts its head: don't apply the aids too strongly and clearly ask less. Prepare the hind legs individually and ask for movement one by one, sitting quietly the whole time. Carry your hands forwards and always ride from back to front.
- The quarters drop out: drive evenly and simultaneously with both legs, keep the horse straight and ask for the upwards transition on the track. When it is obedient to the leg then you can try the exercise off the track and on the circle.
- The horse responds slowly or hesitantly: more mental preparation is needed, check your seat and improve your position. Try riding the transitions out of leg yield with only a small, 30 degrees angle.

A horse will make exactly the mistakes that the rider causes.

Variations

- On a straight line: on the track/on the five metre line/over X from B or E/up the centre line or across the diagonal.
- On a circle or serpentine.
- Walk – canter transitions (refer to simple changes).
- Walk – trot or canter from halt: practice this every day for 10–15 times, but do it three times more on difficult rein!

My tips for success

I have learnt that it is very important to approach every day's work with motivation and to pay attention to the detail. By practising transitions every day this gives me the knowledge that my horse will obey the aids asking him to go forwards without discussion or debate. The rider should be able to manage without needing spurs to clarify what the aids are asking of the horse and without getting into an argument. It is all down to giving the aids sensitively, in the right measure, meaning that the horse is asked to respond at the right moment, in the right place. By doing this, I avoid wasting unnecessary energy and instead have plenty of time to concentrate on harder exercises.

It is better to ride five good transitions than 10, of which only five are any good! With a success rate of 50:50 the horse doesn't learn anything. Less is more. Accuracy is what is required, not mindless repetition.

Downwards transitions – in training and competition

An exercise that comes up again and again is the halt. Whoever calls himself a rider will work hard at reaching perfection, in other words, "collecting" the horse's legs up together whilst maintaining suppleness and looseness in the horse. Both are rewarded when the transitions

A halt can only be performed well when half halts have been correctly used to prepare for it.
Photo: Tierfotografie Huber

halt and "full" halt. A series of half halts are used to prepare the horse for a new exercise or transition and also the halt itself. The horse is contained by applying all of the aids, driving the horse forwards off the leg into the hand until it gives though the mouth and poll (remember the piping bag example). This allows the impulsion from the back through to the front and back again. This improves the horse's expression, attention and throughness.

During my time in Vienna I grasped for the first time how a really well ridden transition is done and what it feels like. A seven-year-old Lipizzaner with powerful quarters helped me with this. I only needed to allow his energetically dancing hind legs forwards into an evenly holding hand and catch the energy with my quiet and straight seat. The whole movement felt smooth from shortening the reins, through to using my seat and the resultant transition. The gelding had especially good basic paces but also had a long back, meaning that it was especially important that I rode him forwards into my hand using plenty of transitions during our daily training.

Prerequisites

To improve the beginnings of collection and the smoothness of movement with half halts, the horse needs to be supple, in rhythm and have a soft, even connection to the rider's hand. I have always paid careful attention to the horse's straightness, since the straighter a horse is, the more effective the hind legs become during good transitions whilst the horse's body is strengthened.

Description of the exercise

What we will call an accomplished or competition halt is the result of a correctly executed training halt. The ideal competition halt should go like this: the rider should push the hind leg

are fluid and easy. The shoulder is lightened since the hind quarters come through under the horse, lifting the weight off the front. We differentiate the half halt, which prepares the horse, from the aid used to actually bring the horse to a stop out of any pace. In German they make this differentiation by describing the two aids as the "half"

After warming up, the horse should be asked to engage its quarters whilst maintaining a good contact. The back should round up under the rider.

through and up into the rider's holding hands with both legs flat against the horse's sides. At the transition the rider's calves should be slightly moved back. The horse comes up into the rider's hands and meets resistance and should give through the poll and mouth gently. Only then is the impulsion from the quarters turned into an ability to carry itself.

In the case of a correctly ridden training half halt which is balanced between the fore hand and hind quarters the horse will increase its freedom through the shoulder and smoothly flow down into the next pace. Every half halt and halt that is executed correctly coming from behind will improve the positive tension through the horse's body that is needed for it to perform movements properly. Summarised, this means that the hind legs are picked up, the back stays loose, swings, is balanced with the rider working discreetly but effectively to maintain the balance together. The forwards impulsion should

be caught through the seat to start to slowly start the beginnings of collection. The training halt gives the rider more time. Together with his horse he can play with and learn to understand the aids in combination with each other, experimenting with how they work in slow motion. At the start of the transition there is nothing wrong with it running on a bit – five to 10 metres if necessary. It is important, though, that the horse is balanced throughout, continues to go straight and comes through from behind and that the hind legs carry the weight. The horse should maintain a good rhythm while the stride length is shortened through the rider's seat. Only then will the horse begin to "dance". Until the moment when the quarters come through to meet the resistance of the seat and hand, the hand needs to stay still and quiet. It holds but may in exceptions become a bit stronger and take up more contact, but should always be released as soon as possible. Never take without giving!

Once the horse is standing square, give softly with your hands. Photo: Tierfotografie Huber

the girth to engage the quarters and stay there throughout the halt. The rider's balanced seat, pelvis and extended upper stomach muscles catches the forwards impulsion from the hind legs. He needs to continue pushing the horse up into a holding hand. Once the horse is standing square the hand immediately needs to soften.

If the halt was prepared and carried out correctly then it should be easy to ride on. A lot of leg shouldn't be necessary.

During the "full" halt aid, the horse should never lose the positive tension through its body. Your touchstone should always be that the horse's movement before the aid is applied should remain soft and loose, so that the horse can carry out the transition without stuttering or delay. The outline of the head and neck should also stay the same while the hind legs are pushed smoothly through from behind up into the seat

In the case of both the half halt and full halt, the degree of activity created, i.e. the amount of "driving" energy created and given by the rider, is of paramount importance. This shouldn't be overdone, though, since if too active an aid is given then the extra speed will be felt through the hand. You need to push the horse up into the hand but keep the energy within the horse, without making it faster. It should come through from behind up into the hand. In correctly ridden halts the rider will find that he will achieve an even deeper seat.

When we change from a pace into the next one down we talk about riding a "simple" transition. These should therefore be easy to ride.

The full halt aid will bring your horse to a halt from any pace and is prepared by using a series of half halts. The legs are applied lightly behind

Be careful that you practice how to apply the correct aid to halt on a daily basis. Try not to always ride with spurs and try to feel what you are doing!

Here, too much hand is clearly being used. The horse has fallen on to its forehand instead of engaging its quarters.

The more thoroughly you practice the training half halt, the faster the horse will learn what collection is and accept the aid asking him to collect. The result of all this effort is the ability to carry out a smooth halt within a shorter distance whenever asked. If the correct application of the aids isn't practiced, then the temptation will be to use the hands more and force the halt, resulting in the horse falling onto its forehand in halt. Many riders think that this is what is meant by a competition halt.

Don't force it! You need to gymnasticise the horse's entire body after establishing a common language. This helps to avoid misunderstanding.

The correctly ridden halt aids described above can be differentiated from the "emergency" stop, which should be taught to every youngster through the use of simple aids as well as the voice. This will serve the safety of the rider and the horse in difficult or scary situations when schooling at home or when hacking out, in case the normal aids aren't yet secured.

A well ridden horse allows the rider to really sit "into" the horse. When the horse fluidly lifts his hind leg to bring it through, it will pull the rider into an upright and loose seat whilst sitting up. The rider should become a part of the horse, rather than sitting on top of it like a clothes peg. The rider should feel the hind legs moving underneath him, the elevated forehand through the lifted shoulder and the wither coming up to meet it. The horse will look as if it is moving uphill, whilst at the same time the freedom through the shoulder should improve as will the horse's cadence with apparently more or bigger paces.

When asking the horse to move more forwards and come through more from behind it will feel as if there is a stool behind you that you could sit down on. The stool will always follow and will be shoved under you from behind bit by bit as you improve the transitions and collect your horse.

This horse is starting to bend his hocks more and come into self-carriage. Photo: Tierfotografie Huber

This drawing shows how the horse's frame shortens in collection. The hocks are clearly bent. Drawing: Philippe Karl

Develop a feel for the way your horse engages his hocks. When training, close your eyes and feel what is happening. Try riding without stirrups.

How do you tell if your training is effective

Thanks to the important gymnastic value of transitions, the ability of the horse to work through its back and hocks will be improved. The hindlegs will move through more underneath the horse's centre of gravity and the hocks will see a greater degree of bend. The horse will look as if it is shortening through its body and will look more collected. The horse will lift its forehand whilst it lowers its quarters. It will be able to carry its neck and head better, whilst maintaining a steady contact to maintain the energy within the horse's body. The horse will appear to move up into the rider's seat without having to use a lot of power or energy. "Think it, don't sweat it" should be your training motto!

The horse's relaxed back should round up more due to the tensing of the stomach muscles. At the same time, correctly ridden halts and half halts will use and strengthen the back and stomach muscles when the exercise is repeated often enough. Main topics of discussion in dressage, throughness and softness, can be trained by using frequent transitions. Its success can be seen in the amount of time that can be saved and the long-term health of your horse.

No half halts means no sparkling horse!

Not a successful transition. The horse transitions down onto the forehand without no engagement from behind.

Problems and solutions

- The horse falters, falls onto the forehand and drags his quarters: sit up straighter and rebalance yourself, move more with the horse through your hips and try riding several trot-canter transitions.
- The horse isn't stepping through straight, but falling out sideways, wavering on the line: straighten the horse, think of putting the forehand in line with the quarters, ride slightly shoulder-fore and then halt, but on the track with the support of a fence or wall, until horse and rider understands the exercise.
- The transition lacks rhythm: take longer to shorten the steps. Halt and then immediately ride on. Think ahead about what you are doing and be ready for the new rhythm.
- The horse goes against the hand and doesn't halt: ride on a circle and ask more forwards, using more seat and less hand.

- The horse hollows his back: the rider is using his back too much as well as putting too much weight through the seat. (Be careful as this can cause horses to strain and damage their hocks!). Sit up straight! Ride varying tempos, pushing through more to engage the horse's quarters more and allow it to dance.

Variations

Transitions are of central importance to the ongoing training of horses and appear in a number of variations, such as "extended canter – collected – flying change or piaffe – passage – canter".

- Transitions on the circle or curved lines: ride on a circle; serpentine; shoulder-in; after or before a volte; on a circle at B/E with transitions. The horse will find transitions easier when going into canter or trot on a circle or serpentine since it will be bent more through its body. The rider will find it easier to feel the movement of the inside hind and can give the signal to canter when he feels the inside hind swinging through with relatively little effort. To move into trot the rider must have the horse in front of his seat and give the signal to trot with both legs.

- Transitions on straight lines: on the outside track; on the 5 metre line; on the B-E line; down the centre line; across the diagonals.
- Transitions when changing the rein: change out of the circle through trot and walk; serpentines; trot – walk – trot; canter – walk – canter. As described above, the rider should only have to use his seat to give the correct aid and keep the horse in front of him. The desire to move forwards should be maintained throughout. The rider needs only prepare the transition well, i.e. shorten the trot or canter strides, give a training half halt, ride on straight for a horse's length and change your rise. Following a balanced half halt the horse should find it easier to trot and canter on. This is also how the simple change in canter is ridden
- Half halts on all lines ridden with canter-trot-canter transitions: to canter ensure the horse is on your aids and is waiting for the next instruction then give the aid to canter with your inside leg. Allow the horse into canter, feeling the quarters come through, sit quietly, ride shorter canter strides and then at the right moment change down into a balanced trot, finding the new rhythm immediately. For walk – trot/canter-walk transitions, firstly, keep the horse sensitive to your leg, shorten the stride then stretch, breath in and trot on. To move back into walk again, shorten the trot movement through your legs, sit into the movement and drop back into the four-beat rhythm, sitting passively. Trot-counter canter – trot-canter: take up trot, shorten the steps, give the aid to

counter canter, sitting very straight and keeping your balance. Then shorten the canter stride and drop back into trot, riding on in the new two-beat rhythm. Shorten the stride again, ensuring an active hind leg and give the aid for canter again with the inside leg.

- Changing tempo within the pace on straight and curved lines: the horse should lengthen or shorten its walk, trot or canter strides but remains in the same pace. Prepare for the extension using half halts, asking the hind legs for more engagement. Make certain that you ride the horse forwards and upwards into the extension, stopping the forwards-driving impulse at the appropriate moment and keeping the horse between the legs and seat. To slow the tempo push the hind legs through up into your seat. The horse's outline through the neck shouldn't shorten. After shortening the stride, ride forwards again.
- Halt from walk, trot and canter: you should be able to halt from all paces, aiming to eventually being able to halt on the centre line. The driving aids need to be maintained whilst shortening the stride. The degree of collection asked for is dictated by the level of training. Don't force anything!

Advanced variations

Each one of these variations has a specific difficulty, which can be perfected with targeted training.

- Riding a 10 metre volte in canter at B or E change the rein over X through walk. This improves longitudinal bend, smoothness and suppleness on both reins.
- Riding a trot or canter half pass, transition back into walk and then ask for trot/canter again. Use half halts especially when the horse tries to rush off to get its attention.

- Start shoulder-in then ask for lengthened trot strides and then either halt or move back into shoulder-in. This will improve the horse's attention to your aids and its suppleness by riding a straight horse into the extension and then collecting again. A further option is to ride so that the impulsion from the lengthening goes into the shoulder-in and elevation.
- Trot shoulder-in – walk but keep to shoulder-in: The horse puts more weight onto the inside hind leg during the transition and can be ridden more uphill. Use all of your aids to contain the horse.
- Ride from half pass into medium trot across the diagonal or on the inside track and then back to half pass. This increases the horse's sensibility. Medium walk–collected walk–extended walk: ensure soft, flowing transitions while sitting quietly. Your upper body should be straight, and when asking for extended walk make certain your own body keeps supple and moves with the horse's movement.

My tips for success
Again and again I notice that too little attention is paid to the transitions. They are even explained incorrectly by many so-called instructors. They concentrate too much on using the hand in the half halts that can have painful consequences for both the horse's body and mouth. Often they are done as an obedience exercise and the horse is taught to respond in a programmed way (as if the horse was a dog being taught to sit and stay). This hasn't, however, any benefits for training but only negative effects. Just using the reins will cause a horse to tense its back and lean on the rider's hands. When a half or full halt is carried out correctly it involves the horse's entire body.

It is the best way to prepare for collection, improves the ability of the hind quarters to carry weight, strengthens the back and improves the contact.

I like to compare the physical demands made by this collecting exercise with the exercise done in gymnastics called the duck waddle. Try it yourself and crouch down low and try to waddle ten steps forward whilst keeping your balance.

You will notice that the closer you get to the perfect half halt, the more your horse will trust you and its body. You shouldn't need to use force or strength. Ride lots of easy transitions.

If you are patient and learn to ride downwards transitions correctly, then you are not far from being able to piaffe. A correctly ridden trot-walk transition is the best preparation for piaffe work.

Lengthening and shortening – changing tempo.

Every dressage rider wants to be able to show off his horse's ability to extend. A horse's natural movement can only truly be shown carrying a rider and saddle when it is fully balanced between the forehand and hocks and when the horse's training is advanced. A four-year-old horse will show good movement and paces but can't yet keep its balance with a rider on its back. It will fall onto its forehand and is difficult to lift up. If trot and canter extensions are ridden too often

Extended trot with active hind legs. Photo: Tierfotografie Huber

for too long with incorrect balance, a horse's working life span will be markedly shortened. The vet will be called frequently to treat problems relating to backs and the forehand and there may be long periods of time that the horse is off work due to strains. The ease with which a horse can lengthen will be lost by practicing in the wrong way. Horses will begin to resist and the rider has to use more power to get the same results.

A horse I rode once that was only 16 hh gave me the chance to experience truly extraordinary paces. The little chestnut gelding had a natural trot extension that was wonderful and could be easily asked for at any time. In his case, the most important aspect of his training in terms of working on this extension was ensuring that he kept his soft and slightly long back supple and rounded. Otherwise, it was virtually impossible for the rider to go with his trot. It was only by

riding a semi-shoulder-fore prior to lengthening that kept his back short enough to keep his softness. Bringing him back was easy with a light hand because he was very sensitive to the leg. Even today at 19 years old he is still competing at advanced level in Japan.

Prerequisites

A basic requirement for riding changes of tempo correctly is correct application of the half halt. There is a constant albeit swinging connection between the horse's hocks and its forehand. The horse may be in balanced self-carriage but the back is active.

Description of the exercise

To prepare for lengthening the horse should be asked for shoulder-fore (refer to page 83), be straight and contained by a half halt. The rider gives a signal from his driving legs on the girth so that the horse steps from behind through to the front into the hand. This creates positive energy and tension in the horse's body. The horse is brought back to collection with an even contact, swinging back and smooth hand.

The straight horse will engage his hocks smoothly so that he is taking larger steps but maintaining the same rhythm with his hind feet landing well underneath his centre of gravity. At the same time, the rider will be pulling the rider into a deeper seat. Even when extending the horse should remain under some tension and take the rider along with its movement. The horse should be light in the hand and shouldn't get heavier either during the extension or the return to working or collected paces. The rider allows the tension that has been built up in the horse evenly to escape through lightly carried hands without allowing his own upper stomach muscles to relax.

By incorporating lengthened strides into your training programme, especially together with the work done to strengthen the horse through its hocks and back, the changes within the pace should remain consistent and rhythmic. The shortening of the stride after lengthening in which ever pace you are working in should follow in rhythm with the beat of the individual pace. The hocks should remain engaged under the seat. Before, during and after the transition, the rider should continue to drive the horse evenly with his legs . The rider will develop a deeper seat and remains in harmony with his horse's movement so that a harmonious picture is given.

Don't forget to use shoulder-fore as preparation!

In a well-thought-out training programme changes of tempo within a pace are pleasant and easy to ride. The rider will develop a good, deep seat and he will find it easy to keep his seat balanced, since the entire series of movements will be fluid and always uphill.

How do you tell if your training is effective?
This exercise will help to improve the horse's impulsion, cadence and the engagement of

When asking the horse back, after lengthening, half halts will engage the hind leg. The contact should stay soft. Photo: Tierfotografie Huber

its hocks. It will learn to come back from lengthening with suppleness and ease. It is sensible to only lengthen for short stretches at the start so that it remains easy to go back and forth in and out of extensions, and to turn impulsion back into an ability of the horse to carry itself on its hocks. Lengthening and shortening the strides will help to secure the horse's throughness with the horse's enthusiasm being taken into the collection. The horse will become elastic in its movement and will remain enthusiastic in its work.

Problems and solutions

- The horse falls off its line: traighten up and sit evenly, lengthen on the outside track and only ask for short stretches.
- The balance between the horse's forehand and quarters is lost when lengthening or shortening: ask for less in terms of effort and distance, the rider may have asked at the wrong time or too much. Apply your aids better and with more coordination.
- The horse goes against the hand: the rider may have tensed through the reins, causing this tension to run into the horse. Therefore, use less hand and more leg. Ride shoulder-fore or work on a circle.
- The horse hollows his back: the rider is using too much seat and back. Ride some simple transitions keeping the horse contained, asking with your legs into your seat. Then start again.
- The horse is losing rhythm: the rider himself to stay in rhythm and move with the horse, applying your leg aids in time with the horse's movement.

Variations

- Straight lines: diagonals/go large/down the centre line/ B-E / other lines.

- Curved lines and circles: half and full circles/ circle at B/E.
- Use other schooling figures in combination, such as half 10 m circle in the corner at canter, counter canter then lengthen to centre line and half circle back to the track in collected canter.
- Halt – rein back – medium trot.
- Ask for lengthening around the corners from A/C to the corner markers without changing the rein.
- Spiral in on the circle then make it larger: this helps collection and bend when making the circle smaller. When enlarging the circle ride almost shoulder-in and ask for lengthened strides. When extending strides, keep sitting on the horse's hind legs and keep the croup low.

My tips for success

I can see that the work is having a truly gymnastic effect – and that is, after all, what it is all about – when

- the hind quarters are showing lots of forward thrust and the hocks are bending deeply,
- the horse's back is loose and rounded up in positive tension under the saddle,
- there is plenty of freedom through the shoulder,
- the head and neck are in self-carriage.

Only then is the entire horse engaged and improving all of its muscles working effectively together. We must expect the horse to be able to work almost silently at all paces. It is a great joy to me when I come into school and see all of the horse's working quietly almost like ballet dancers. Unfortunately, you more often see a battle forming between rider and horse, which is usually down to the technical ability (or lack thereof) of the rider (poor seat, hands held too high, double bridle done up too tight) to restrict the horse. Often the stronger forehand movement hasn't been evened up with the weaker movement from behind. The back stays hollowed and this doesn't allow the quarters to really engage through into the hands. Very rarely do you see a correct extension, which should be swinging through the body from behind.

Only when you pay attention to keeping your centre of gravity with that of your horse during lengthening and shortening, will you avoid the horse falling on its forehand. At the start you should ask for less lengthening over a shorter distance. Use all of your aids to ask the horse to shorten up again but be quiet and careful, especially with your hands and avoid pulling or taking a hold on the reins. You should practice this combination of aids again and again in short bursts.

If you get this right then it will become so much easier to capture the horse's forwards impulsion and use the impulsion in the collection. Here, too, I like using an analogy: just as squeezing a tube of toothpaste by mistake can lead to its contents spurting out, out of control, so can the horse's energy be lost or go out of control by riding a change of tempo incorrectly. You need to pay attention and work carefully on your medium trot!

Develop the extended work gradually and then really feel when the horse collects again. Keep things harmonious. Careful work will save you vet's bills. „Extended trot and not expensive trot!"

Counter canter

Counter canter gives an indication of the training level of a horse. The counter canter can be helpful to show a horse and rider when they don't already know, how a more collected canter should feel.

Shut your eyes and try to feel the physical tension running through your horse's body. What are the hind legs doing? When and where are they landing and leaving the ground?

The first time I tried counter canter with a four-year-old mare of mine that had amazing paces, she not only did it, but then did a beautiful flying change in the corner. I had to think how I should react because if I allowed her to do it, any time that she lost her balance after that in counter canter she would change legs. In the case of this mare, I started instead with some gentle and fun work on flying changes and only later when she had developed a more controlled and dynamic canter did I work on a balanced counter canter. Today, of course, she can do both.

Prerequisites
The rider has to be able to ask for canter on both reins from the seat. The horse is capable of maintaining a relaxed and straight canter. By riding plenty of good, simple changes the horse will be more sensitive to the aids, be able to be collected and remain supple. The horse will have learnt to carry itself and is therefore now ready for the counter canter.

If the horse stays on the aids and remains supple and straight, then it is ready for counter canter.

deep into his horse.

With the horse flexed slightly to the outside, the inside leg supports and ensures that the horse's quarters don't fall into the school. This is especially important in the turns. A successful counter canter develops the ability of the horse to carry its weight from behind in tight turns and circles as well. But be careful that the horse's neck is in line with its shoulder and that there isn't too much bend through the neck.

The horse's balance in counter canter should be supported by the rider's weight spread evenly through his seat. It should not be difficult to turn the forehand by using your weight and inside leg. The horse should never be supported by the rider's hand, but instead be in self-carriage and positive tension through his head and neck.

Keep your horse's attention! Remain very straight through your body and don't lose your balance.

Description of the exercise

The counter canter is nothing but a correctly collected canter done the other way around, with the leading leg to the outside not the inside. Half halts are used to prepare the horse, and the rider uses his inside leg to activate the inside hind to start the canter. Don't overdo it, but give the signal and wait. Allow the first canter stride forwards so that the inside hind steps through underneath the centre of gravity. This will only happen if the rider is sitting balanced in "positive muscle tension" and allows his inside hip to move slightly forwards in the direction of the movement. The better a horse learns to carry itself in counter canter the better a rider can learn to sit

How do you tell if your training is effective?

This exercise has a strong straightening and collecting effect. In addition, due to the exercise involving cantering from walk, halting and rein back it places greater demands on the horse's hocks, requiring them to bend and engage. The canter in counter canter will become more polished and freer through the shoulder. At the same time, riding turns, voltes and tempo changes in counter canter will also improve both horse's and rider's balance. Riding shoulder-fore and shoulder-in in counter canter is also an effective way of straightening a horse. When you include in this changes of tempo (i.e. lengthening and shortening the stride within the pace) then this

When you do a difficult movement well, give you and your four-legged partner a break. Photo: Tierfotografie Huber

will improve impulsion and submissiveness. Counter canter helps to engage the attention and interest of both rider and horse. Both find their shared centre of gravity, out of which they can respond to the different demands required in terms of both forwards momentum and collection. Using your reins to transmit aids should become virtually superfluous, since the horse will become so off the rider's seat that the rider should only have to give the smallest of aids through the hand. A well ridden, balanced counter canter is the best way to prepare for the flying change and other more advanced movements.

Counter canter is very demanding and must be done in small doses!

Problems and solutions

- Starting canter on the wrong leg: go back to walk and canter on alternate legs from a calm and collected walk, preparing each time with a softly ridden half halt.
- The horse changes legs in canter: do a series of simple changes to get the horse more on your aids, trying spiralling in and out on the circle and containing the horse clearly with your outside leg and asking for consistent collection in short stretches.
- Horse is falling out through the outside shoulder: ask less with the inside rein, hold more with your outside leg but make sure that the leg is not too far back and that you are sitting straight but in the direction of movement, leading the forehand slightly to the outside with both hands and seat.
- Horse loses balance: check the rider's seat critically, ask for a quieter canter, making sure the rider's outside leg is always on the horse's side.
- Losing tempo and falling back into trot: counter canter for shorter stretches, and include lengthening down the long side.
- Canter is crooked: move the horse's forehand off the outside track whilst keeping the quarters out on the track. If the forehand tries to

If your horse is balanced correctly in canter, then the counter canter will also be balanced and straight.

move across, use your aids to keep it on the outside track.

Variations

- Prepare for counter canter by riding a loop down the long side in canter. This allows you to practice turning the forehand in, keeping the loops shallow.
- Change from the corner marker to B/E (small diagonal), out of the corner half circle and back on the track, or change from circle to circle. By not changing canter lead you auto-

matically move into counter canter as you change direction. Use your seat, that should be absolutely still, to change the direction of the forehand.

- Do the same as above but starting from counter canter, moving from canter to counter canter and back. You can also ride voltes.
- Ask for counter canter from walk, halt or rein back. This will show how well the horse is collected and through.
- Ride down the centre line in counter canter, circling to left and right in canter and counter canter. Make certain that the circles are balanced and come back to the centre line.
- Three to six loop serpentine without changing canter lead: This tests the ability to change direction around the serpentine holding the balance of both horse and rider.

My tips for success

When, in the course of training you get to the point where you begin to work on counter canter, you will find that you will use this exercise again and again to help to improve collection and straightness. The hind legs should follow along the same line as the front. Any problems with rhythm or self-carriage will solve themselves when you can maintain an active canter in self-carriage (up hill) supported through the rider's seat. The rider's hand should notably play a lesser role so that the horse concentrates on the feeling through its body and isn't fixated "mentally". Take care horse and rider don't over exert themselves physically or mentally working in counter canter. Practice the movement in doses small enough to keep the horse motivated but not too large that the horse gets bored.

Flying changes

When you reach the stage of starting to teach the flying change, your horse should be well balanced. Even young horses who are naturally gifted with a good sense of balance can start to play with flying changes at this stage, for example, when doing jumping exercises. Even at this stage, though, the rider should from the start insist on the hind leg coming through together with the opposite foreleg, so the change is "clean". This will mean that later when changing legs in the collected work there won't be any, or as many, problems.

For horses that find it easy to change the lead in canter, you will be able to build in flying changes to change direction with no great problems. If the horse has natural balance and a good canter then it is possible to build in flying changes – correctly executed, of course – to the warm-up phase for fun.

With my horses I always find that they really enjoy learning to do flying changes. In one instance I had a very quirky little pony in for training that was very strong-willed. It clearly showed me when it was ready to start canter changes, otherwise it would have made its own decisions in terms of direction and tempo. In this case, it was exceptionally important to train systematically: without the work on flexion and suppleness you couldn't get any further, since the pony's balance was too strongly on his forehand and my hands. I always started every lesson with simply transitions on a circle, moving up into simple changes through canter. Only then when the pony was really listening and accepting my aids, could I start on flying changes. At the beginning of every session then I would ride one or two flying changes.

For flying changes the horse must be absolutely straight. Photo: Tierfotografie Huber.

Prerequisites

To do flying changes the horse has to be able to work in a relaxed and rhythmic canter without rushing. The rider should be able to shorten and lengthen this "uphill" and well-balanced canter easily. The rider knows the aids and should be able to control every stride.

If the flying change is done correctly don't forget to praise him! Your horse should remember the things it does well. Photo: Tierfotografie Huber.

leg, to rest flat on the horse's side. What was the inside leg will then become the new supporting outside leg to keep the quarters straight.

What is important is that the horse remains in front of the rider's seat throughout! The seat must remain quiet and balanced so that the horse doesn't wobble and stays straight throughout the changes. A stronger contact will be produced on what was the inside rein. During the change this will then become the leading and straightening rein. The new inside (was the outside) rein allows the change by giving through the rein and should become lighter in the contact. Changing the flexion through the neck is absolutely the wrong thing to do, since it leads to a loss of balance! The neck should stay straight and act as a balancing aid.

Imagine that you are riding on a balance beam: canter straight – change straight – move on straight ahead.

Description of the exercise

Before asking for the flying change the rider has to understand the theory, in other words, what actually happens during the movement. He has to sit absolutely upright and have a good connection through the reins. The horse must be straight. The outside hind has to be prepared for the change over as it will later become the inside hind. To do this, the rider's outside leg will press two to three times in time with the horse's leg leaving the ground. Then the rider will move what was the outside leg forwards but without applying pressure, to become the new inside

How do you tell if your training is effective?

The flying change will motivate both horse and rider, will make the horse more sensitive to the rider's aids and will wake it up, serving to also help develop impulsion. In addition, the taking up and releasing of weight through the hind legs, alternating from one to the other, that are also being asked to step more under the horse's centre of gravity, will all help to strengthen the horse's stomach muscles – the horse's "bascule" – and will improve its suppleness.

When the rider and his horse are in perfect balance together then the flying change doesn't require any effort; it is much more a case of the

Working on flying changes is fun for both horse and rider and builds strength in the hind quarters.

rider releasing an expressive change from his horse that is cantering in tensed anticipation of the aid. Providing that the horse is cantering uphill, then if done correctly the horse should be able to proceed in the same rhythm. Neither the balance nor the horse's self carriage should be lost. By gradually reducing the strength of the aids throughout your training you should be able to produce more lightness and more elegance in the changes.

Think of a water pistol: fill up, pull the trigger, release and canter on!

A successfully ridden flying change is easily recognised by a number of obvious characteristics:

- The horse becomes more uphill and shows more expression.
- The horse jumps through clearly uphill in the change and remains in balance, with the canter showing a certain positive tension.
- The change "releases" itself forwards-upwards with impulsion.
- The horse waits for the rider to ask for the change and is concentrated on its job.
- The horse remains straight into the new outside rein.
- During the moment of suspension, the horse changes its legs underneath a well, rounded back, which also helps to improve both its suppleness and the tension through its body.
- The rhythm and fluidness of the canter should be maintained unchanged before, during and after the changes. The horse should process in a regular canter without rushing.

• The rider sits quiet and straight to hold his balance and applies his aids quietly and subtly.

Canter rhythmically –
don't rush!

Problems and solutions

Co-ordination problems are often experienced with flying changes:

• Rhythm is often lost and often the horse doesn't jump through cleanly with its legs: change tempo, go back to circles and practice counter-canter without changes.

• You lose balance in the turns, the rider's seat becomes unbalanced and he gets that "motor-cycle round the corner" feeling: sit up more, ride voltes in collected canter whilst sitting up straight.

• The horse loses its balance between the fore-hand and hind quarters, the canter is too quick with the croup too high: before starting with changes collect the horse to ensure that it is in self-carriage, use less leg and prepare the horse better by using half halts.

• The horse gets crooked: make sure you have an even contact through both reins and use counter canter to straighten the horse.

• The horse is positioned too much in the direction of the movement: use the diagonal rein aid, i.e. on the "wrong" side, use less hand and keep the horse absolutely straight using the new outside rein.

• The horse changes through late: ride a series of tempo changes (extensions and shortenings) to re-establish impulsion, suppleness and col-lection, do lots of simple changes and secure the leg aids by doing lateral exercises (refer to page 83) but don't be too forceful. A problem with changes through the forehand is a problem of wrong hand aids, don't change the flexion through the neck!

• The horse doesn't change at all and doesn't react at all: go back to simple changes, be clearer with your aids and insist on a reaction, don't try to "carry the horse" with your hands, do lots of changes of tempo from collected to extended canter and back again on the circle.

• The horse anticipates the aid and puts a change in before being asked: ask for flying change coming out of half pass or counter canter. Less is more so only practice once or twice and stop at the right time and reward the horse for doing well.

• The horse starts to rush: this can be caused by a number of things. 1. The aids aren't coordi-nated correctly. Solution: do lots of simple canter changes on the long side, practice the aids, with the legs always applied in the same place and ask for canter with the inside leg! 2. The rider is putting the horse under too much pressure. Solution: ride more from your seat and leg. 3. The rider is not sitting quietly. Solution: stay quiet through your body, keep your hands down and apply your leg correctly.

All problems need to be analysed carefully for their causes, since that is the only way to find the right solution. The training over the previous weeks and months should be looked at and checked. Look for rider weaknesses on a daily basis and correct them yourself.

Mistakes due to your hands are ten times as bad as other mistakes!

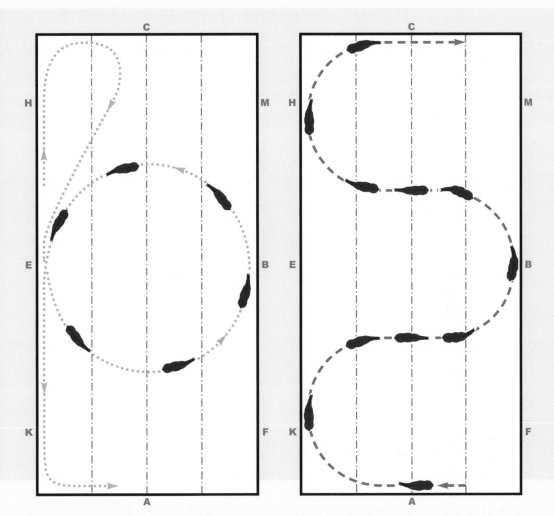

Change the rein out of half circle into counter canter, circle at E/B and do a flying change on the circle.

Three loop serpentine with a flying change when crossing the centre line.

Variations

Once flying changes have been learnt they can be integrated into a variety of other exercises:

- Ride a half circle from the corner marker to change the rein in counter canter and then ride a 20 metre circle at E/B with a single flying change: keep the horse together, and release the energy through the change.
- Three loop serpentine with flying changes when crossing the centre line: after riding the

turn with good bend, you will need to react quickly to straighten up for the change; the old inside rein should lead.

- Change the rein across the full and half diagonal (K-M/F-H or M/F-E, H/K-M) with flying change before and on reaching the track: keep the collection, sit in the middle of the saddle and keep the horse in front of your aids.

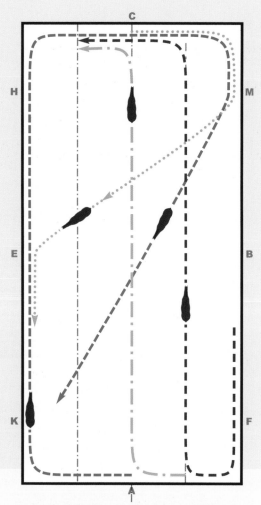

Blue line: change the rein across the long diagonal with a flying change when reaching the track.
Orange line: change the rein across the short diagonal with a flying change when reaching the track.
Green line: flying change on the centre line.
Lilac line: flying change on the five metre line.

- Medium or extended canter, collect and change: collecting the canter sits the horse on its quarters and engages the hind leg, the shoulder is freed up and the change can come through.
- Ask for a flying change when riding down the long side on the centre or five metre line: this prepares the horse for tempi changes (a series

of flying changes with a given number of strides between each change).
- Flying change in medium canter: keep the tension through the horse's body, maintain a fluid uphill canter using half halts to alert the horse to the changes and maintain control.

My tips for success
Flying changes aren't particularly difficult for horses. Out in the field they will do them by themselves just for fun. Under saddle, though, with the added weight of a rider on their shoulders, they will find them considerably harder to do. Horses with exceptionally good natural balance and a naturally uphill canter are able to do flying changes even with a rider at an early stage. This can be a real advantage when jumping or hacking out. If the horse learns, though, at this early stage to do a "Show jumper" flying change, meaning that the inside hind comes through late, careful work will need to be done on the action and readiness to collect of the hind legs to cure this problem. Bad habits can be difficult to cure. At the start, one good flying change is enough. The horse should be rewarded straight away and allowed to relax. A well ridden change is more effective than doing three, of which only one is correct. When you can really feel what the outside leg is doing and use signals beforehand to prepare it for the change, you will then be able to engage it with virtually invisible aids. Try to feel the impulsion and the development of power that this exercise brings with it. Keep the horse straight by holding with the new outside leg, not driving. As soon as the horse understands the exercise, you can reduce the aids to a minimum. I always pay attention in my training that I either do flying

changes correctly from the start or put them to the end. With horses that are perhaps more difficult in temperament I give them plenty of time and design a very individual training programme, as the problem is normally not doing flying changes, but there are other weaknesses. These need to be recognised and fixed before you can proceed with the training.

Pay particular attention to the side of the horse that is more difficult to ride straight, since from experience this causes more difficulties. Ride straight first of all then try again. If misunderstandings occur between you and your horse when learning flying changes, then stop, go back a step and start again. Voltes and simple canter changes will help.

Checklist for riders:
- Have I prepared myself and my horse correctly?
- Have I applied my aids at the right time, in the right quantity and in the right place?
- Am I sitting in balance?
- Am I holding my hands quietly?

How do I teach the flying change?
1. Teach the horse how and then practice (ride fewer but better flying changes!),
2. Train (using lots of different exercises and variations),
3. Do them at every possible marker (when and where you want to).

We need to design a horse's training programme individually according to its age, temperament and level of training. How we proceed will also depend on our own level of training. Using a combination of all of the lessons learnt up to this point, I am always able to put together new, varied training options to motivate our horses. By taking short breaks during training this allows what has been learned to sink in and rewards the small successes, such as listening to and waiting for the rider's aids.

Rein back

The natural direction for horses to move in is forwards. You do, though, sometimes see the horse moving backwards in the field or in the wild. This usually has something to do with defence, attack, resistance or subordination. As riders, we can use this exercise to check whether the horse is submissive to the aids, and when the horse is more advanced in its training, it can also be used for collection and to get more flexion through the hocks. Rein back should never be ridden without careful preparation. It should only ever be used as a correctional exercise at critical moments when the horse forgets who the boss is. The rein back helps to call the horse to order and then you continue on with what you were doing without any further fuss.

For me, the rein back comes into my training programme fairly late on as it assumes a submissive and relaxed horse. If it is to be used to improve collection then we would need to move it into the next chapter.

I particularly remember a mare, that didn't find rein back difficult at all. She did tend, though, to escape away from my aids which were asking her forwards by going backwards. In her case, I avoided reining back as an exercise for a long time, since this bad habit was difficult to cure. Even now I have to ride this movement

A correct rein back can always only be ridden out of a correct halt. Photo: Blacky

with care: she has to always be clearly in front of the aids and must never be asked to rein back with the hand.

Prerequisites

When working on the rein back it is always important to ensure that the horse is able to supplely move in balance whilst maintaining a regular contact in all three basic paces. A further condition is that the horse has been trained by half halts to move from behind through into a contact and accepts all of the rider's aids, both to move forwards and to collect. Acceptance of the aids to halt is also especially important.

Description of the lesson

First of all, you need a balanced halt, in which the hind quarters are asked to step well underneath the horse. Once the horse is standing square, allow it to chew on the bit and maintain a degree of tension through your seat in the horse's body. The rider should sit up straight with his upper abdomen out slightly so that the horse is kept together and could be ridden forwards at any moment. Thanks to the horse being slightly uphill and the resultant openness of the shoulder, the rider should be sitting deep. The rider shouldn't need to use any strength to get the rein back. The backwards steps should be diagonal in a regular two-beat rhythm. To get this, the rider needs to apply his legs on the girth to drive the horse up into his hands to create the right degree of energy. So that the horse steps backwards the rider wraps his legs around the horse's tummy slightly behind the girth. After practice, this movement of the legs slightly backwards should suffice to get the horse to move back. Until it reaches this stage, though, rhythmical giving and taking alternate reins should be enough to ask the horse to step back

For the rein back, the horse must stay more in front of the seat.

on diagonal leg pairs. The rider should initially sit still and use little, if any, seat. The training level of the horse will determine the degree of collection and the flexion through the hocks. At the start you can also sit slightly forwards to take some of the weight off the horse's back.

If the horse responds then it can be allowed, at least in the initial stages of learning, to hold its neck in the position that is most comfortable for itself – usually lower. The submissiveness to the driving and holding aids is most important here. Later, when the horse is able to put more weight onto its quarters, it will be expected to rein back from a more raised forehand off a rider's seat and leg with more flexion through its haunches. To end the rein back, the rider puts his legs on the girth again as if he wants to move forwards. Thus, what was a holding or supporting leg becomes an active one. The horse is allowed to move smoothly forwards by asking the hind leg that last landed on the ground to step forwards again. If the rein back is to be ended in a halt then the horse should take a last half step back to stand square and on the aids.

It is a positive result when the horse accepts all of the aids willingly and without question, thus really communicating with the rider.

The rider's seat has to maintain the same degree of tension from halt throughout the rein back so that he can ride forwards at any time. It is wise to ask for only a few steps at first, only increasing the number of steps after practice when you are more sure of the exercise.

How do you tell if your training is effective?

The gymnastic effect of the diagonal sets of legs stepping backwards is very valuable. It helps to teach the horse a degree of self containment and also strengthens the ability of the horse to carry itself. The centre of gravity is moved back and so prepares the horse for the more collected work of pirouette and passage, which asks the horse to take more weight down through its haunches. Greater sensitivity comes also with increased collection. The horse will also more willingly respond to lighter aids.

Problems and solutions

- "Creeping back": the horse is trying to escape from the rider's aids by creeping backwards. The rider needs to ride more full halts and half halts and then ride energetically forwards. Forget about rein back for now and instead make certain that the horse moves off an active leg.
- "Shuffling" back: the legs need to lift off the ground and step back more energetically, so the rider's legs need to be more active on the girth and only ask for one or two steps then

ride forward in trot. The horse should be encouraged to go in self-carriage, so prepare more using half and full halts so that the horse improves its balance and develops a more uphill tendency.

- Hesitant and against the hand, resistance shown through the reins and with a raised croup: check the bit and use less hand with clear leg aids asking the horse forwards. Keep the horse in front of the seat, otherwise, stop trying instead ride different tempos within the pace.
- Rushing back: use your leg actively and insist that the horse listens, use less hand and work on simple transitions and changes of pace.
- The horse isn't moving its legs in diagonal pairs: go back to riding transitions, have lots of patience and then be satisfied with a few, correct steps back. If the horse refuses to go back, it may help to ride the steps slightly laterally and keep the steps calm, don't let it become hectic.
- The rein back is crooked: keep the horse straight through its back and check that your full halts are effective. The horse should stand square and straight before moving back, with the rider placing even pressure through both legs, with reins the same length and the weight distributed through your seat evenly and centrally.
- The horse tries to rear: ride with your head and with feeling – really think about what you are doing before you do it! Ride forwards and forget about reining back altogether. Avoid getting into an argument or being tempted to use force!

Variations

- On the outside track
- Anywhere on a straight line in the manege
- Rock (back and forth): from the rein back go

immediately into walk without halting, then after four steps, again without halting, ask for rein back.

- Change the length of strides: depending on the degree of collection, ask for smaller or larger steps.

My tips for success

The rein back is a highly effective exercise when done correctly. Experience has shown me, though, that rein backs are rarely ridden correctly. At competitions you will often only see the hesitant, creeping back variety of rein back that appears to have been drilled into so many horses. This can be seen by the marks left in the surface from the horses dragging their feet back, rather than picking them up! I start to prepare my young horses for this exercise in-hand. Once the horses have understood the aids (body language, whip, voice and hand) with me on the ground, I can then more easily and with lighter aids work on their sensitivity to the aids and the beginnings of collection. I will work on rein back by lightly touching the horse on the chest or front leg. However, this should always be done with the horse moving forwards and never too often so that the horse doesn't get bored or overstressed. Initially, you should be happy with even just one step, as long as the legs are moving diagonally. This in-hand work can always be done parallel with all of the other ridden exercises that you are doing, such as straight lines, leg yielding, transitions or giving the reins and allowing the neck to stretch.

The most effective training exercise is a combination of riding forwards and backwards, like a swing would. From forwards you ask for the rein back and then from backwards movement ask the horse to step forwards again.

Walk pirouette, turn on the haunches or demi/half pirouette.

At this stage of training the rider should be able to see a clear refinement in the way the horse accepts the aids and thus in the degree that the rider is able to apply the aids. It is now time using the walk pirouette to check whether the horse is really fine-tuned to all of the aids. The pirouette will help to show this asking the horse to actively pick up and place down each hind leg.

Prerequisites

The rider should be able to ride simple transitions and understands how to activate the hind legs individually whilst keeping a relaxed rhythm (alternating pressure with the legs in walk, be aware of the four-beat rhythm!). He is also aware of what a supporting leg and forwards, driving leg aid is. In addition, there should be an understanding of the diagonal aids, as, for example, used with shoulder-fore.

Description of the lesson

The walk pirouette, more often ridden as a half or demi-pirouette and also known as a turn on the haunches, can be used to change the rein using shortened walk steps to link two sets of movement. The forehand is moved around the haunches, always keeping slightly ahead of the quarters. The forehand describes a larger circle, whilst the quarters describes a smaller one, with the forelegs crossing over. The hind legs keep walking, stepping up and down, albeit without crossing over! The horse remains in a four-beat walk rhythm with the hind legs stepping through more underneath the horse's relaxed centre of gravity.

In preparation the horse is ridden straight but with a more lifted forehand from the shoulder.

The walk steps are shortened, however, moving with purpose by the rider's hand being more held in place, but all the time staying soft. The pirouette begins with the horse being flexed and bent correctly in the direction of the movement. The forehand is asked to turn by the rider moving both reins slightly sideways and the outside knee and thigh asking in the direction of the turn. The outside calf supports and limits the movement of the quarters whilst at the same time controlling the outside hind leg. By alternating the driving leg aids from one to the other throughout the turn the hind legs are encouraged to keep moving in time with the walk. Both hind legs should step around in a small half circle and the flexion of the hind legs should be improved.

While the upper leg still controls and limits the forehand, the bend and flexion is maintained until the half pirouette is completed by reaching the track, assuming you are doing the exercise on the outside track! At this stage straighten the horse, ride forwards and ask for the new bend. When starting this exercise it is totally acceptable for the hind leg steps to make a larger circle but it is important that the rider keeps his aids consistent and not apply them too strongly. If this is done then the horse will trust him and will feel well contained. The horse should be in self-carriage and not rush through the movement.

Throughout the entire half pirouette the rider should maintain a relaxed three-point seat. Despite activating the hind legs the horse's body should remain, in effect, on the spot, held through the rider's seat. Thus, the created energy is transformed into more carrying power of the hind legs. The rider should clearly feel both hind legs stepping underneath him. Before starting the pirouette in walk, trot or canter may be ridden, and then immediately after the pirouette the horse can be ridden forwards into the pace that it came out of.

Another variation of the pirouette in walk is the turn on the haunches. This begins from halt. After the halt, pause a few seconds and then ask the horse to take a step forwards into a half pirouette. On completion halt again. A turn on the haunches demands more precision and faster application of the aids. This exercise is done particularly well by horses that are more self-motivated and forwards-going, in other words, those that by nature have an active hind leg and will bring a certain "freshness" to the exercise. Other horses will need to be motivated to keep the hind quarters active and engaged by the use of the correct aids and multiple transitions.

The canter pirouette is similar in both the execution (the line the exercise follows) and the aids. The rider's seat remains the same, but the effect of the seat comes out of the rhythm of the canter. The outside leg has to be stronger in its action. The inside leg repeatedly asks for the canter stride, keeping the horse going but without allowing it to move forwards. The rider's seat has a decisive role in this, i.e. centring the horse and keeping the quarters on a small circle through the use of the rider's back and abdomen.

Your horse will respond to clearly applied aids! Then turning the forehand, "dancing" hind legs and self-carriage will become easy for both of you.

How do you tell if your training is effective?
During the pirouette the horse should take more elevated and more rhythmic steps. With consistent longitudinal bend it should take more weight down through its quarters. Self-

carriage, flexion of the hind legs and the ability to collect should all see improvements. The action of the forelegs stepping across forwards and sideways has a gymnastic and suppling effect on the horse's shoulder. The horse's entire body works supplely under the rider's centre of gravity. The balance between the forehand and hind quarters, along with the rider's weight is optimised. The aids for the half pirouette need to come without delay but never be rushed. For the rider, this means that he is required to apply a complex combination of aids and will learn to direct the horse's shoulder whilst shortening the stride through the hind legs that have to kept active, all at the same time. This can go so far as to almost being piaffe-like steps.

Problems and solutions

- The quarters fall out: before beginning the pirouette make the quarters more sensitive to the outside aids by riding almost in travers.
- The pirouette becomes either too small or too big: the rider has to be able to control the speed of each individual step, with the regularity of rhythm and flow maintained throughout. The size of pirouette will depend on the level of training.
- The forehand won't turn: come into the pirouette in shoulder-in and end in a clear shoulder-fore.
- Rhythm is lost, becoming either too fast or too slow: ride a larger pirouette and by clearly asking the horse forwards, keep it in front of the rider's legs. Divide the pirouette into four quarters and after every quarter ride forwards so the exercise is separated out into short sequences. Come into the pirouette in shoulder-fore.
- The hind legs stay in place and don't move round: you may be using too much hand or poorly applied half halts. Apply your legs in time with the walk.

Easy to see: In the half pirouette only the forelegs cross over, with the hind legs stepping in time with the walk.

- Flexion and bend is lost: ask for a larger pirouette circle and make certain that the shoulder is always leading. When you lose bend, come out of the movement and go back to basics such as circles, voltes and lateral exercises.
- The horse comes off the line of the movement, becoming a "turn around the centre": the horse is not on or in front of the aids. Get the horse more sensitive to the legs aids to either side by riding some lateral exercises. Get the horse in front of your seat by riding a quarter pirouette and then immediately moving into trot or canter.

The more supple and loose the horse is, the faster and more willingly it will learn all its lessons!

81

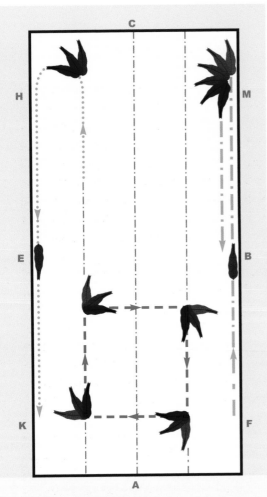

Blue line: the square pirouette.
Green line: quarter pirouette towards the outside track.
Orange line: half pirouette, although it can also be done slightly larger.

Variations

- Square pirouette: begin with the horse facing the track. Ride a quarter of a pirouette and then ride straight ahead, followed by a further quarter pirouette, and so on. The horse is alternately collected and then ridden forwards. This keeps the horse agile and attentive.
- Full pirouette: start by riding a "working" pirouette with a much larger radius. The flexion and bend remain constant with a slight turning

of the forehand. Only start to reduce the radius of the pirouette when you can maintain rhythm and impulsion throughout.

- Ride off any and every straight line, on and off the track: always start the pirouette with a hint of shoulder-in and end in the same way, changing pace out of the movement to keep the steps fresh.

My tips for success

When working on pirouettes I always concentrate on the logical sequence of the main points of the movement:

1. Understand the line, preparing by practicing square pirouettes.
2. Ride into it with a hint of shoulder-in and end in the same way (refer to the following chapter).
3. Ride large pirouettes: start with working pirouettes and learn to really feel what the hind legs are doing.
4. Constantly check and activate the hind quarters – then ride pirouettes with a smaller radius.
5. Always ride the movement until it is completed.
6. Start to prepare for canter pirouette by riding half pirouettes within simple changes.

This exercise has a lasting effect on rider coordination and the application of the aids. Being aware of sitting centrally is just as important as having independent hands. When carrying out the exercise correctly it should suffice to give the aid, keep your body positively tensed and carry your hands so they frame the horse. Riders often forget about the hind quarters and the need to get them to step up and through at the right time – without this the movement can't be done. Correct preparation prior to the pirouette and half halts are the basics that determine the quality of the pirouette.

Lateral movements

The lateral movements are effective training exercises where the horse is ridden with flexion and clear longitudinal bend on two or more tracks. The lateral movements improve the flexibility of the entire horse's body. You don't just ride them for the sake of it, but rather because they are some of the most important suppling and gymnastic exercises that there are. They help to strengthen the horse's abdominal muscles that criss-cross under the stomach, which, in turn, has a positive effect in relieving the muscles over the back.

At the same time, this work has a positive effect on the shoulder and hips by increasing their suppleness and mobility as well. The straightening effect also helps to develop the ability of the inside hind leg to carry more weight, which in turn frees up the shoulder allowing it to become more elastic. The crossing over of the outside hind across the inside also supples the haunches and improves their ability to carry the horse and develop impulsion.

An apparent contradiction: riding with bend encourages straightness.

Riding travers, renvers and half pass also has many positive effects on the horse's body and health. These exercises are also good for horses that have problems with suppleness or may not go as relaxed as is wished. In this case, you can kill three birds with one stone: develop a greater awareness for the horse of its body, supple the horse and start to develop collection. How this happens will be shown in more detail in the training plan that is detailed later.

Shoulder-fore – riding in position

Straightening the horse is the most basic exercise that a rider continuously has to do, since horses are by nature crooked! If we allowed the crookedness to remain as it is then we couldn't sit on a horse's back. If, however, we want to be able to ride a horse, then all four legs have to bear the same amount of weight and the hind legs need to follow in the same track as the forelegs. Only then can we say that the horse is going straight.

The "magic" exercise for straightening is the shoulder-fore. The narrower forehand is adapted to the slightly wider hindquarters by bringing the shoulders out slightly so that the shoulder, together with the inside foreleg, is brought onto a line with the inside hind. What may sound obvious turns out on closer inspection to be something working against a basic physical fact: by nature the horse is naturally crooked to the left or right.

If this crookedness isn't evened out then too much weight will fall onto the diagonally opposite foreleg. The opposite hind foot will not step under the centre of gravity but instead to the side of it. If this isn't fixed then this crookedness will mean that the rider's weight isn't evenly distributed. However, if the weight can be distributed evenly over all four legs, using training designed to do this, then the horse will be able to balance out its own and the rider's weight. It will suffer less wear and tear on its limbs and back. This is especially important now when our horses tend to be larger and have bigger movement! If the horse is straight in the shoulder-fore, then you can start to work on the lateral movements. Through the gymnastic effect of the straight, bent horse (i.e. a horse that is straight but ridden on curved lines) comes gentle collection.

Prerequisites

The rider must be co-ordinated and have the horse on the aids. The rider can control his seat and apply the aids correctly, also being able to control the resulting response.

In the second position – here ridden on the opposite or counter rein – the outside hind leg needs to step through in a line between the front legs.

Description of the lesson

The shoulder-fore comes out the exercise of riding the horse in a flexed position. The first position is ridden with the horse bent evenly through its length on one track, but with the inside hind encouraged to step more underneath the horse's centre of gravity. The rider pushes this leg forwards as it take off to move more towards the forelegs. At the same time, he needs to maintain a constant contact from his shoulder through his hands and down through both reins. He needs to drive with the inside leg so that the inside hind swings through into the rider's hand so that it can be felt. The rider's outside leg supports the hind quarters.

In the second position the horse stays bent through its length just like before and remains on one track. The outside hind leg as it takes off should be held on the track by the rider's outside leg but again encouraged to step through more. The inside leg works to keep the inside hind moving forwards towards the inside fore. It is important to carefully apply the legs in the correct measure from a seat that is slightly turned, the rider's seat and hips needs to swing through with the movement and there needs to be a constant and even contact through both reins. There is less contact taken up on the inside rein as soon as the horse is moving flexed in position.

Once this exercise is understood by both horse and rider, you can begin the work on shoulder-fore. This is ridden on a single track and combines the first and second flexed positions as detailed above. Using a slightly turned seat, the outside thigh and both reins carried lightly to bring the horse's shoulder out slightly in front of the rider's inside hip. Picture the horse's outside foreleg landing in the middle of the track and the inside fore on the inside edge of the inside track. Due to the preparation that the rider has under-

A correctly ridden shoulder-fore with active hind legs.

taken with riding in flexion he should be more aware of what the horse's hind legs are doing and be better able to control them. He should be able to ensure that the hind legs stay on a narrow track and step like being on a beam. By straightening the horse the rider should be able to ask the hind legs to come under the horse so that the horse steps shorter, but doesn't lose its bend. Be careful that the horse's neck doesn't angle out more into the school or become deeper. The shoulder should be controlled with the outside rein at the withers.

Riders should now notice a further improvement in the suppleness and strength of the horse's back (functioning like a bridge between hind quarters to the front). If the quarters are engaged then the movement should flow from the back through to the front into a quiet hand. In both lengthening and shortening of the stride in shoulder-fore the horse should move smoothly and rhythmically in balance. In Steinbrecht's words: "ride your horse forward correctly to straighten it".

> Always ride from a balance seat so that the horse can step through under its centre of gravity.

How do you tell if your training is effective?

Riding in flexion has a gymnastic effect on each of the hind legs, suppling both the inside and outside leg and prepares them for later collection that will ask the hind legs to carry more of the horse's weight. As in the case of all lateral movements, here the horse will also appear to become shorter through its frame and the hind legs should appear to dance, lifting its shoulder and making the horse easier to turn – like a car with power steering. The more a horse is worked towards collection, following the scales of training, the more sensitive and attentive it will become to the rider's aids.

The less energy a rider has to use, the less energy the horse will also need to expend. This is particularly significant when it comes to working through the harder movements. Greater collection required in more advanced training (piaffe, passage, pirouettes or halting on the centre line from canter) has its foundation in the shoulder-fore. By using a correctly executed shoulder-fore as preparation, movements such as a balanced medium trot or a well executed half pirouette should take care of themselves and flow easily. Changes of tempo within a pace will help with impulsion and sparkle when working on straightness. In addition, horses will gain in expression and will continue to enjoy their work.

Riding a horse that is trained as well as this will be an unforgettable experience in terms of the harmony found in its movement by the rider. As a rider you will get an exceptionally smooth ride, since the horse can and will swing through his whole body.

Problems and solutions

- Falling out through the outside shoulder: apply the outside aids more. Turn your outside thigh in, close the knee and give with the inside hand. Contain your horse more.
- Too much angle: too much inside rein is being used so give more with the inside hand and use your seat to contain the horse.
- No bend: go back to working on a circle and on the first and second position.
- The horse is running on in front: the rider may be sitting crooked. Ride without stirrups and try to feel where the central point is, keeping your seat quiet and drive less, and more con centrated through the seat. Push through more from the inside leg into the outside hand.
- The horse is crooked: too much leg is being used on one side. Ride less angle until the horse moves more smoothly and use your leg to contain the horse.

" Less is more" is one of my most important principles when training! Ride more precisely and feel what the hind legs are doing.

Variations

- Go large, circles, centre line, quarter line: always think of the shoulder-fore and feel for the inside hind.
- Going large and half circles: come out of the corners with shoulder-fore that is moving forwards well then in the middle of the long side turn onto a 20 metre circle and ride the horse deeper into first and second position. Try doing turns with the horse lower in its outline and stretching in the neck.
- Counter shoulder-fore – shoulder-fore towards the outside of the school: this can be very useful with horses that are heavier in the hand. Both horse and rider will have a greater awareness of the outside aids, with the horse flexed and bend to the outside and its forehand towards the outside of the track. The quarters should be fixed by the rider's outside leg to the inside of the track.
- Ride through the corner in shoulder-fore, maintaining impulsion throughout: keep the horse clearly on the inside aids. Ride into the corner pushing through from an active inside leg into your outside guarding leg and hand that supports and stops the horse from dropping out. Immediate, turn the shoulder in and ride out of the corner with the outside leg.
- Ride shoulder-fore before, during and after a demi-pirouette: ride into the movement in shoulder-fore and keep thinking of the shoulder-fore throughout the exercise. Often, the

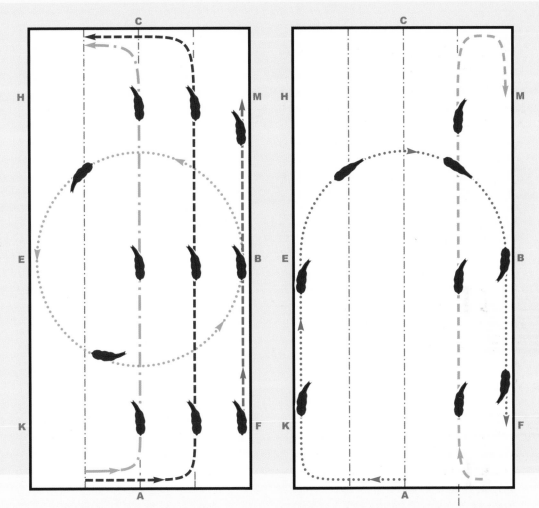

Blue line: shoulder-fore going large.
Green line: shoulder-fore down the centre line.
Orange line: shoulder-fore on a 20 metre circle at E/B.
Lilic line: shoulder-fore on the quarter line.

Blue line: shoulder-fore going large, then ride straight onto a half 20 metre circle, then back to shoulder-fore.
Green line: shoulder-fore to the outside.

preparation into shoulder-fore is neglected and the exercise itself doesn't work.

- Come out of shoulder-fore and do two half voltes, then back into shoulder-fore: this combines bending and loosening with straightening and collection.
- Shoulder-fore down the centre line – figure of eight at X – shoulder-fore down the centre line on the other rein: this asks for straightness on a

line off the track and then two voltes with a change of rein, followed by shoulder-fore on the same line again. This will make the rider more aware of his outside aids and will he be aware of any problems through not being able to hold the horse on the correct line.

- For advanced riders, try riding half pass in shoulder-fore. When starting to work towards half pass, you start with shoulder-fore. Keep the horse's shoulder in the same position during the flowing exercise as well. Keep thinking of shoulder-fore and make sure that you ride it as well.

My tips for success

As soon as you are sitting on your horse's back it is your job to secure the stability of the horse's body underneath you. Of considerable significance in all of this is the need to compensate for the horse's natural crookedness. For this reason, you need to continually think about and ride shoulder-fore as soon as you are on your horse. Don't forget to first of all ride the horse straight as you should always ask a straight horse to bend, otherwise you stand the risk of getting too much bend from your horse. This will mean that the stiff side will stay stiff and will lead to the horse's joints suffering too much wear and tear. At the same time, the supposedly better side, which is actually weaker, will be put under more strain. By overdoing it on this side you can cause lameness through the shoulder.

Riding in position with an active hind leg is the first exercise that you should ride on a daily basis as soon as you get on. Even in the simple shoulder-fore version of this both horse and rider will be made more aware of exactly to where and when the hind legs should be moving. This will help to ensure that the horse always goes with the correct flexion and bend. Regardless of what level of training they are at, I always ride all my horses slightly shoulder-fore so that I am always prepared to ride any movement correctly, whether this be shoulder-in down the centre line, medium canter on the quarter line, walk and canter pirouette or piaffe from shoulder-fore. I have ascertained that

this enables me to work through the straightening and collecting work much more efficiently and faster. I reach what I am trying to achieve in my training with less effort and without overtaxing my horses. Think of being in a gym: when you are working out, your fitness routine is carefully thought out and worked through. Starting with fewer repetitions the muscles are warmed up and given a work out but not over stressed or stretched. Carrying out the exercises incorrectly can lead to strains, inflammation of the joints and even chronic pain.

In just the same way you need to start slowly with the straightening and bending work with your horse. Take plenty of breaks during training but gradually, week by week the hind legs and quarters are slowly and gradually prepared for increasing levels of collection, such as moving from canter to halt to piaffe. These exercises should be done as a kind of interval training: alternate straightening exercises with loosening work, changing the tempo and regular breaks.

The shoulder-fore needs to be ridden for weeks, months and years. It is the best training exercise to even up a horse's one-sidedness as well as helping to free up the shoulder and keep its movement smooth and rhythmical.

Shoulder-in and counter shoulder-in

The shoulder-in is the mother of collection and all of the other lateral movements. With this movement both horse and rider will reach maturity. From now on you should use this movement on a daily basis at varying angles of flexion and bend, in other words, varying the degree of difficulty. It is interesting to see how much this exercise can change the course of a lesson. After a shoulder-in a horse usually has more impulsion and better paces than before. Try it yourself!

During a course I was giving I remembered that this movement could also be done as a "counter" movement (the opposite way around) and by introducing this quickly gained the attention of both the riders and their horses. By incorporating counter shoulder-in, often forgotten about, down the long side, it immediately helped to improve all of the participating horses' submissiveness, ability to take more weight onto the quarters and self-carriage.

All of the exercises that then came out of the shoulder-in worked as if by magic. In the case of working canter, counter canter and flying changes, I saw more concentrated and cooperative horses. The riders themselves noticed real progress and were aware of forming a real partnership with their horses. To achieve this all I needed was half an hour. In this time we were able to bring all the horses a huge step further by structuring the work properly but without a great deal of effort. The riders also noticed that their aids became much simpler to both apply and be understood. With little effort they completed a successful training session that they could then repeat at home.

Prerequisites

The horse needs to be able to happily work on circles and curves and can be correctly ridden through corners. It should be able to work correctly in shoulder-fore and allows itself to be bent around the rider's inside leg, showing a moderate degree of angle of the head and neck.

The horse should be moving through its back well, a light poll and chew gently on the bit. The hind legs should follow in the same track as the forelegs. The rider will have a well-balanced three-point seat and is able to control every part of his body independently. He should be able to feel when his horse's hind legs are leaving the ground.

Description of the exercise

Increased collection begins with the shoulder-in. In comparison to the shoulder-fore, the shoulder-in is ridden with more angle, with the forehand lifted up more and with more bend. Its level of difficulty is dictated by the angle at which it is ridden. The horse will go either on three tracks (an angle of 30 degrees) or four tracks (45 degrees). The greater the degree of the angle and bend, the more weight the inside leg has to bear.

When riding on three tracks, the forehand needs to come far enough into the arena so that the outside foreleg steps along in the same line as the inside hind. When riding on four tracks the outside fore and inside hind leg each go on their own line. The outside fore steps on the second track and the inside leg on the third. Regardless of the degree of angle both hind legs should move straight ahead on their own track and never cross over. The fore legs, on the other hand, should cross over slightly but keep a good forward momentum.

Before starting the exercise, use half halts to get the horse's attention and engage the hocks. The well-balanced rider, when starting the shoulder-in, should put more weight into his inside seat bone briefly as if wanting to start a volte. As soon as the horse turns in, the rider gives a half halt, pushing his upper abdomen against the movement. At the same time, he maintains his central balance through his seat. The inside hip needs to move with the horse's hips as the inside hind comes through.

It should be easy to increase the angle of the movement and go from shoulder-fore into the shoulder-in.

The rider needs to sit very straight, keeping his upper stomach muscles tensed. Imagine sticking out the part of your tummy that is above the waistband of your jods. The rider needs to move his inside shoulder slightly back, so that his shoulders are parallel to the horse's shoulders.

The rider should push through from his inside leg to the regulating outside hand, with the straight seat catching the momentum to help the horse sit back and carry itself more. At the same time, the outside leg, upper thigh and outside rein contains and controls the horse. The inside leg that is on the girth encourages the horse's inside leg to keep actively forward and moving underneath the horse. It also helps to encourage the horse to flex through its poll.

The now attentive horse should be flexed and slightly bent to the inside. It is brought in with both reins and the outside upper thigh as if the rider was asking for one eighth of a volte. The rider needs to use the reins like the handlebars of a bike – the outside rein goes slightly forwards and allows the shoulder to move through. At the same time, the rider keeps the horse flexed to the inside and when the horse turns in immediately become lighter through the inside rein. The outside rein controls the action of the inside hind leg.

To finish off this exercise the forehand needs to be moved back onto the track in alignment with the hindquarters, using the upper thigh, the inside hip and the inside leg on the girth pushing the horse back out. At the same time, the rider needs to move his shoulders back in line with his hips and sit briefly against the movement, taking both reins across to lead the horse's shoulder back onto the track. Finally, the horse needs to be ridden straight forwards into shoulder-fore on a good contact.

During this exercise, combining as it does bending, straightening and collection, the rider should have a constant, well-centred seat. He should be able to sit easily on his horse that is moving with purpose, with his legs wrapped around the horse's sides. The connection between the hand and the horse's mouth needs to stay elastic and light.

Assuming that horse and rider are in balance, the exercise should be completed with the horse in self-carriage.

Shoulder-in should only be asked for as long as the movement stays light and easy. Repeated often over short stretches combined with bending and collecting work will have a positive effect on training, but only when you ride forwards between the exercises.

Now we turn out attention to the counter shoulder-in and how it is performed. The horse should be ridden on the quarter line with the forehand angled towards the track. The bend, position and collection should stay the same as with the conventional shoulder-in. The aids from the leg are as required for the level of bend and angle and the inside leg (which is now on the same side as the outside track) should be on the girth. Keep the horse's attention by applying the outside legs intermittently. When you turn into the counter shoulder-in the rider's weight needs to stay briefly to the inside, towards the track and then is followed by the aids as for the shoulder-in. Counter shoulder-in can be ridden on any straight line and to increase the difficulty can also be ridden on circles.

How do you tell if your training is effective?

The reason this exercise is so effective has already been explained in the shoulder-fore work, which is the predecessor of the shoulder-in. Due to the different variations in angles that the shoulder-in offers, the degree of bend and collection can be increased noticeably. As well as improving the ability of the horse's quarters to carry more weight (through the flexion of the haunches), the stomach and back muscles are also strengthened and the horse's self,carriage will also see an improvement. The forehand should be lifted in relation to the lowering of the haunches and the horse should carries itself with positive physical tension through its body. The horse should move through the exercises more fluidly and with more elevation, collection and cadence.

What can we now do with our straight but flexed and bent horse? It allows us to ride forwards with impulsion and collect back easily and without breaking rhythm. We should be able to ride from medium trot to halt without difficulty or turn onto a pirouette from extended canter.

Counter shoulder-in will allow you to work on balance and collection as the horse will be more attentive to your seat and more obedient to the leg.

This can also be used when doing jump training, as the aids contain the horse better and allow for better straightness so that it can be ridden into narrow jumps without concern that it may run out.

You can also ride the counter shoulder-in on four tracks. Consequently, flexion and bend should be increased.

out: ride travers on a circle (refer to page 96)
- You lose the contact or the horse is tilting its head: widen your hands, move your hands forwards slightly and use less outside hand. Try riding voltes between each shoulder-in. Go back to circles and work on suppleness through the head and neck and taking up a constant contact through both reins. Remember, even the weak side of the horse needs to have a good contact. Also, try riding counter shoulder-in along the track.
- The angle is too great: go back to shoulder-fore and ride with more bend.
- The shoulder-in becomes "head-in" – in other words, the shoulders don't move off the track: be particular about asking for constant bend throughout the horse's body and use less inside rein.
- The horse's poll drops too low or is over bent: ask for less angle and change the tempo.

The biggest mistake that is made again and again is asking for too much too soon and tiring the horse. The rider must develop a feel for what the horse is capable of and then draw a line. This exercise can always be done at walk to save the horse from over-doing it. Remember, less is more, so always increase the frequency you ride any exercise gradually!

Problems and solutions

- Uneven rhythm or inconsistent tempo: go back to circles and work on rhythm and suppleness.
- The horse rushes: turn off shoulder-in into a volte and then when you come back to the track start the shoulder-in again.
- Falling out through the outside shoulder: ride counter shoulder-in, using less hand and close your outside leg firmly around the horse.
- The quarters or outside hind leg are falling

Variations

Shoulder-in can be combined with other lateral movement to give you lots of different training exercises:

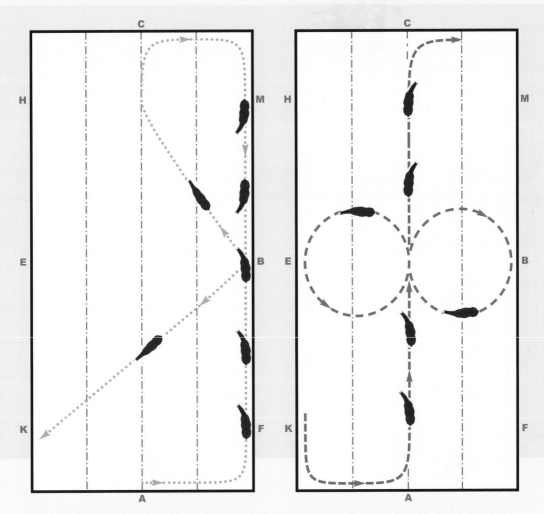

Shoulder-in on the long side, asking for extended strides out of it to the centre line and then back into shoulder-in.

Shoulder-in on the centre line with two voltes and a change of rein.

- On straight lines: ride along the track, across the school and up the centre line.
- Ride on circles and its variations such as spiralling in and out on the circle.
- Ride through the corners in shoulder-in.
- Volte – shoulder-in – volte.
- Combinations such as:
  - Ride a 20m circle at B/E – ride shoulder–in (with the quarters staying on the circle) then go large and ride the next half long side in shoulder-in and then go back onto the circle, allowing the horse to relax then shoulder-in and ride across the next diagonal asking for lengthened strides.
- Ride on a straight line away from the track in shoulder-in then ride a short diagonal and go back to counter shoulder-in.
- Go large in shoulder-in and then ride across the school on a short diagonal line asking for lengthened strides.

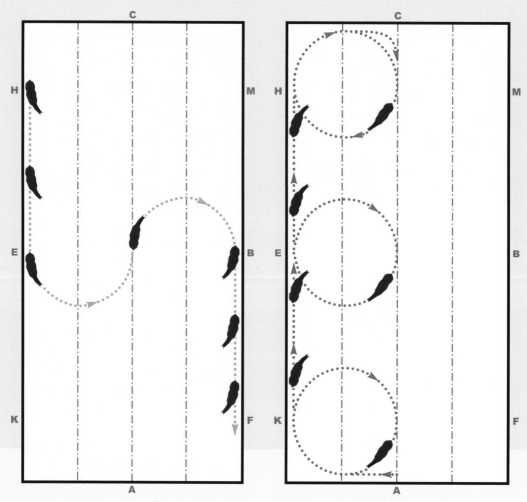

Shoulder-in with two half circles followed by shoulder-in.   *Shoulder-in interspersed with voltes.*

- Ride up the centre line. Ride shoulder-in left, then a volte to the left, followed by a volte to the right and then shoulder-in right.
- Shoulder-in down the long side then at B/E ride two half voltes to left and right (or vice versa) and then return to shoulder-in.
- Shoulder-in down the centre line-half 10 metre circle – shoulder-in down the long side – two half 10 metre circles – shoulder-in down the quarter (5 metre) line.

- Shoulder-in on the track – extended walk across the diagonal to the far quarter line – shoulder in down the quarter line.
- Ride a volte in the corner and then come out of it in shoulder-in – volte – shoulder in – volte – shoulder in.
- Shoulder-in – half pirouette – counter shoulder-in (very useful in canter); counter shoulder coming out of a half circle in the corner.
- Ride on the quarter line in counter shoul-

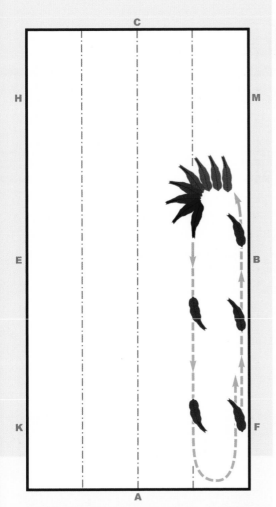

Shoulder-in, half pirouette and then counter shoulder-in

When working in shoulder-in I always notice how important this exercise is in giving horse and rider a feel for collection. In order to keep the horse's (and rider's) attention, you need to work in short bursts, using straight stretches where extended strides are asked for to break up the work, but always keep in the back of your mind what the work is supposed to be achieving. In this movement I place particular emphasis on maintaining an absolutely constant tempo and rhythm. If both are correct then the horse is not evading either the collected or bending work being asked of it. Varied training using the straightening effect of the shoulder-in and the loosening work on circles has proven to keep the horse motivated and interested. If problems do occur then you should immediately go back a step, asking for less angle, shoulder-fore or even a more basic exercise. It is usually sensible to break up the movement with a short diagonal, volte or half circle. This allows the horse to relax for a moment and find its suppleness and looseness, flexion and bend again. You can then go back to the collected work in shoulder-in with a horse that is refreshed and hopefully happy to work with you rather than against you. You will be more successful in your training with a horse that is happy in its work, and the lessons are more likely to "stick" with it.

der-in; ride across to the corner marker on the track, around the corner in a half circle and back to the track in shoulder-in.

Always give your horse clear instructions. Ride with your head!

It is important not to ask too much of your horse, and remember to change the rein often and alternate between working, collected and extended paces.

The wonderful effect that this exercise has is to turn a horse that is moving forwards well with impulsion and swing into an expressive horse that can carry itself. It should literally dance with confidence across the arena with the rider sitting upright and lightly in the saddle. The horse should never be forced into collection, but instead be led towards it gradually as is appropriate for the horse's age and level of training. It should be happy to work through its "fitness and body building" training every day.

After three to six months, training you won't recognise your horse. Horses with a weak neck will now have strong upper neck muscles. Since they have to carry their head and neck correctly, the neck will appear to come more out of the withers in a wedge shape, narrowing as it reaches the poll. The horse's entire top line will have changed for the better.

In the courses that I run I always look at the muscles along a horse's topline to form an initial picture of the training that it has been done with it.

My pupils know that if they follow my training methods they don't just get a horse with a wonderful neck, but that both horse and rider will have fun every day in following them.

Travers, renvers and half pass

When watching travers and renvers, you should see a horse with a good outline moving its forehand and quarters each along two tracks. Compared to the shoulder-in, which required the shoulders to be brought off the track, with this new exercise we ask for the quarters to be moved into different positions at differing angles. The shoulder needs to move along a straight line which always stays on a parallel line to the line of the exercise.

All forms of lateral movements help us to improve the horse's gymnastic ability, outline, suppleness through the back and self-carriage.

Prerequisites
The foundations for a correct travers, renvers or half pass are rhythm, suppleness and contact. The horse should be able to carry out correctly serpentines, spiralling in and out on a circle and turns on the haunches. You should be able to use collecting exercises and changes of tempo to engage the hocks and lift the forehand. Both horse and rider will be capable of doing shoulder-in well and the rider can apply the aids effectively and in exactly the right place at the right time.

Description of the lesson
The travers is a sideways movement in which the horse is bent and flexed in the direction of the movement. It is a collected movement as only then is the horse likely to be able to keep its balance. The forehand is ridden straight along the track with the neck fixed at the withers remaining almost parallel to the track and the forelegs do not cross over, unlike the hind legs. The hind quarters are moved off the track at an angle that is in proportion to the horse's bend. The horse will be moving on four tracks at a maximum angle of 30 degrees.

I would always recommend asking for a smaller angle at first in order to keep the movement fluid and so as not to interfere with the freedom and mobility of the shoulder. The horse should set its hind legs down on a narrower track to the side and forwards. The outside hind steps across more underneath the rider but the inside hind continues to step forwards.

The associated but opposite exercise to this is the renvers. It is very similar to the travers, al-

In travers the forehand is always ridden straight ahead and the forelegs do not cross over.
Photo: Horses in Media

A renver with plenty of impulsion ridden on the inside track. In contrast to travers, it is the hindquarters that are ridden straight ahead.

though this time it is the forehand that comes off the track and is bent and flexed in the direction of the movement. The forehand moves parallel to the track on a second set of tracks. The hind quarters stay on the outside track and step forwards in the direction of the movement. What has been the inside hind becomes the outside hind, held and supported by the rider's outside leg. What was the outside hind becomes the inside hind and is driven forward in the direction of the inside foreleg by what is now the rider's inside leg.

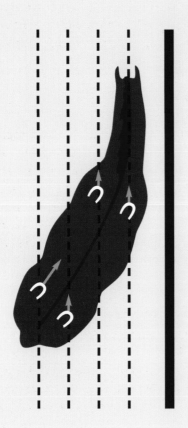 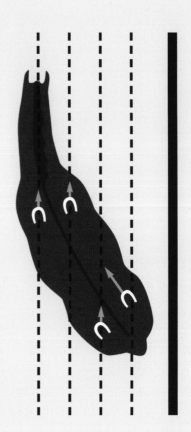

The correct sequence of footfalls in travers and renvers.

In the case of both exercises, the rider sits to the inside at the start of the movement, putting more weight down briefly through the inside seat bone. The inside leg, which should be on the girth is responsible for keeping up the forward momentum and maintaining the bend. In addition, it activates the inside hind leg. With a con- stant contact with the horse's mouth through both reins the bend is allowed through lightly giving with the outside rein. At the same time, the outside rein supports the shoulder and ensures that the neck doesn't bend too much and stays connected with the withers. Using a soft hand it is flexed inside enough that the horse can gently chew on the bit. It is always the forehand that is adjusted to the quarters and never the other way around. Before, during and after any lateral movement, the horse must be able to go off the rider's seat.

It is really only fun to do these exercises when the horse works and thinks with the rider and its attention can be kept with only the lightest of signals. Always work through the half pass in small steps.

Step one:
small travers/renvers
Using only a little collection, but keeping the horse going forwards smoothly, this helps the horse to understand the new lesson. With a small travers the hind legs should come off the track only at a minimum angle but with good bend through the body. It is done as follows:
• Ask for more angle from the quarters on a circle, coming out of the second position (refer back).
• Move into travers at a smaller angle off the circle down the line of the track, keeping the quarters at the same angle off the track.
• Do a pirouette on the centre line and ride travers from there. Use the bend from the half circle but ask for more and then ride straight ahead with the forehand into travers.
• Change the rein into the corner (start by riding diagonally away from the track to the centre line and do a half circle from D/G) and use the bend from the circle to ride into the travers. This exercise is the opposite to riding a half circle at one of the corner markers (FMHK) into

the school, and gets the horse's attention and is excellent preparation for the half pass.
• Three or more loop serpentine: After changing the flexion ride forwards into travers/renvers.
• Shoulder-in – renvers – change the rein into the corner.

Step two:
full travers/renvers
The same again but with more bend, angle and collection. If you lose impulsion ride straight ahead and get back the impulsion and then ask for a little travers/renvers at a smaller angle, maintaining the rhythm until the horse is happy. Your goal should always be to use as little energy as possible to get as much as you can.

Step three:
small half pass and full half pass
The small or training half pass is the same as a travers ridden across the diagonal, with the horse moving on three tracks. At the start the horse is ridden with little angle along the line of the exercise – in this case the diagonal line – to help to secure an understanding of the sequence of the exercise for the horse. The forehand should move exactly on the line of movement towards the corner marker. With time the degree of collection – together with the bend and the sideways movement – should increase. It will then become a half pass on four tracks.

To start the training half pass the horse should be ridden deep through the corner attentive at the inner hind leg and turned onto the diagonal with a clear shoulder-fore position. Once horse and rider are into a forwards-sideways movement then collection and carriage need to be maintained using half halts.

A good example of a half pass: the horse's shoulder is leading, flexion and bend are clearly pointing in the direction of the movement.

Never lose rhythm or impulsion!

The following exercises will help to secure both the small, and the full-blown versions of the half pass:

- Ride across the diagonal in travers, imagining that the diagonal is actually the outside track. The forehand should move straight along the line of the diagonal and the quarters should be brought off the line to the inside in the direction of the movement onto a second track.
- Half circle out of the corner to change the rein and move into the half pass. Ride with the forehand ahead towards the track and then ask the quarters to follow.
- Ride along the centre line in shoulder-in into half pass towards the track.
- Change the rein across the diagonal in medium trot, but after X change to travers along the diagonal and keep the impulsion.
- In canter, spiral in on the circle until you reach the point of riding a working pirouette

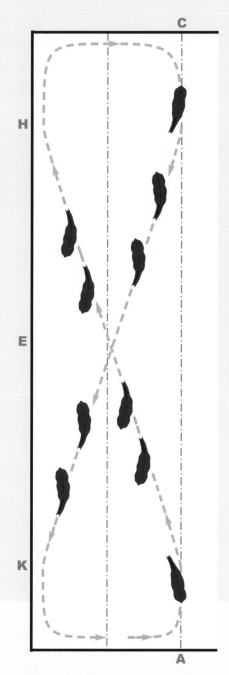

Half pass from the centre line back to the track.

and then spiral out again. Pay attention that you maintain the forwards impulsion when moving laterally!

The rider has to start the half pass with a back that swings and from a seat that is turned towards the movement. A half halt should be ridden to put the horse on the aids and get its attention. Then the rider asks for a shoulder-fore and for the horse to step through onto the inside hind, so that it is in front of the aids.

If this happens, then the rider can ride the half pass with contact through both reins and actively using his outer leg. As the outside hind leaves the ground, the rider asks it to move across forwards and sideways.

The leading forehand is contained by the outside rein in the right position. The inside leg remains on, and is responsible for the balance and forwardness of the movement in what ever pace the horse is in. The movement should become more collected and more expressive and rhythmic. If the horse rushes it needs to be held using half halts and more retaining reins. At the end remind the horse to bring the quarters across using the outside leg and by sitting through the movement. The energy is contained in the horse that will be uphill in its movement, and this could easily be released by asking for extended strides when back on the track.

Once we have learnt the half pass properly, the difficulty can be increased and the sequence of movements varied. Now the lateral movements can really be worked on. Remember that it should be easy to move on forwards at any time when riding a lateral movement.

Step four:
zig zag half pass
On the one hand, the zig zag half pass is ideal for training a change of sideways direction and

In the zig zag half pass.

on the other hand to make the technique more automatic. It should include at least one change of direction. Concentration, submissiveness and collection are all required in quick succession. An exercise leading into this is to ask for several 5 metre half passes back and forth to the quarter line from the track. Increase the difficulty by riding down the centre line and ask for 5 – 10 – 10 – 5- or 3 – 6 – 6 – 3-metre half passes back and forth. By this I mean moving five metres to the left, then 10 metres to the right, and so on.

First ride the exercise in walk and trot. The half pass equivalent has a flying change between each change of direction and so is very difficult. When a zig zag or double half pass is ridden, the rider needs to straighten the horse briefly before changing the bend. In canter this means a flying change. If you don't have your horse on the aids and moving on its own then though you

... the changes of direction come quickly.

might just perhaps manage the flying change, you won't manage the change of direction in the new half pass in the short time available. The difficulty of the zig zag half pass lies in the fact that all parts of the exercise have to be carried out in very quick succession: finish one half pass – keep the horse in front of you in shoulder-fore – change the bend and ask for the new half pass. And throughout you have to not lose your or your horse's balance!

Everything that is easy for us, will also be easy for our horses. One of your goals should be to ride with a seat that is tightened ready but not overtensed. The positive use of physical tension throughout the body is one of the important characteristics of a rider with a good seat, and of a well-ridden horse.

How do you tell if your training is effective?

When working in half pass the horse is stretched sideways. It will learn to flex its joints more and carry more weight through its quarters with greater flexion of the hocks. As a result, more impulsion will also be created. All of the points that are important during a horse's training can be worked on by with the help of half pass: rhythm, looseness, elasticity in the connection between the rider's hand and horse's mouth, impulsion, straightness in the bend and increased self-carriage. It is a first class body-building programme which helps to produce a horse that is stronger with more energy. The half pass is one of the most enjoyable movements to be able to ride with your horse as the improvement felt in the suppleness of its movement feels great! This work also builds on the collection, bend and flexibility started on in shoulder-in. The improved quality of the impulsion is also expressed through the horse's movement, which will have much more cadence. The resulting lightness and energy seen in the movement should be a pleasure!

The rider should be able to sit in the centre of the movement with a broad and relaxed seat in positive physical tension and in total balance. He should be swinging passively with the movement. The mobility of the horse's back is optimised, as is the tension in the horse's body and the forehand should be lifted which, in turn, improves the horse's balance. Achieving the relationship of 1:3 forehand to the hind quarters is getting closer, and it increases the horse's capabilities of doing more. The entire picture becomes more harmonious not just for the rider but also for spectators. The virtually invisible communication that takes place between the horse and rider will seem to be telepathy!

Problems and solution

- Losing rhythm: ask for less angle or go back to basics such as voltes or shoulder-in. Use shoulder-fore to develop greater impulsion.
- The quarters lead: begin with shoulder-fore and think shoulder-fore during travers/renvers and in the half pass. Use less hand and make sure that the inside legs go more forwards.
- Tilting head: the outside hand needs to go with the movement but controls the bend lightly, while the inside hand is put slightly forward. Go back to a large circle and ride the half pass out of this.
- Lacking bend: use the inside rein less, ride the horse more between seat and leg, try to feel the bend. Ride a number of voltes.
- Falling out through the outside shoulder: ask for less angle, and apply more outside thigh and knee while using less hand.
- The horse loses balance: ride shorter stretches of half pass, alternate between forwards and sideways, with lengthened strides thrown in occasionally to break up the exercise.
- The rider's hands are too low at the withers and not flexible: ride voltes on the left and right rein, checking that the rider's hands are in the correct position at the withers and check whether the horse is coming off the seat and leg.
- The rider is sitting in the opposite direction to the movement and collapsing through the hip: go back to voltes, making sure the rider's shoulders are parallel to those of his horse. Practice riding on the volte without stirrups to encourage the inside leg longer and the inside hip more forward.
- The rider's inside leg is too far back: ride shoulder-fore or shoulder-in, making sure the inside leg is forward! Serpentines will also help horse and rider ride with the correct bend.

- The horse isn't tracking up enough: ride shorter, steeper angles in the lateral movement or take a break and go back to the start.
- Half pass to the right and left are different: a horse's natural one-sidedness can never be totally overcome and you will only ever be able to get close to achieving identical work on both reins. You will find that the "good" and "bad" side changes in the course of training.
- The end of the half pass isn't clean: it is particularly important to ask the horse to move its outside hind across with your outside leg. Use half halts to keep the horse's attention, or when you reach the track ride a transition down, repeating this several times.

Variations

These series of exercises will help to improve mobility, sensitivity, balance and submissiveness:

It is sensible to change the rein frequently so that you don't risk straining the horse's hind legs. Overtraining can lead to you making backwards, not forwards progress and can leave a long-term indelible negative mark on a horse. Bad experiences can be difficult to erase, being saved as they are on the horse's "hard drive". To undo this, the negative influence has to be totally erased and then the horse has to be taught all over again from scratch.

- Travers/renvers on a circle, then canter when coming off the circle: this gets the horse's

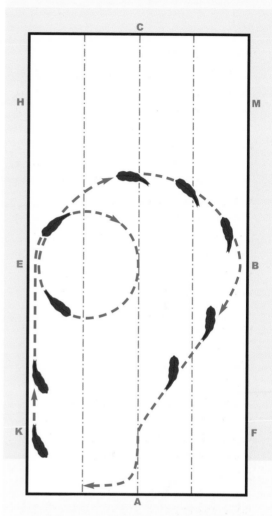

Travers immediately followed by a volte, then shoulder-in on a half 20 metre circle. This can be extended by adding a short half pass to the centre line.

attention, strengthens the outside hind, improves collection and demands more mental agility.
- Travers – volte – shoulder-in on the circle: this alternates training on collection from one hind leg to the other.
- Change the rein out of the circle, doing travers then renvers: working on the inside hind, then

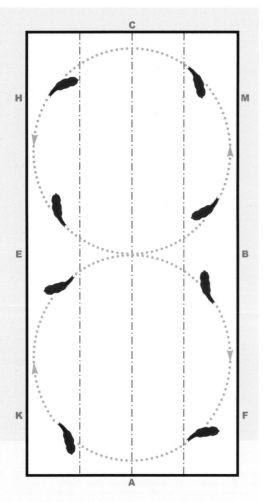

Travers on the circle, change rein over X then renvers on the circle.

- Starting on the long side ride travers/renvers, ride through the corner and onto the centre line to X then turn back to the track.
- Travers – half pirouette – renvers: the rider keeps the horse's flexion and bend in the travers with his aids throughout. Trot on briskly straight after.
- Change the rein out of the corner in a travers-like position but reduce the size of the circle as you come onto the half 10 metre circle, as if you were spiralling in on a circle: this will help when you start work on canter pirouette.
- Shoulder-in – renvers: strengthens the horse's mobility and alternates the weight carried on one then the other hind leg. At the same time, the horse's bend has to be changed and the rider has to change his seat in the opposite direction.
- Change the rein, riding in renvers from the long side (between E/B to the corner marker) onto the centre line and back into the corner, then half pass off the corner: in preparing for renvers the feeling for the bend is developed and the horse's shoulder will be better felt and controlled.
- Renvers on the diagonal – half 10 metre circle at the corner marker to the centre line to change the rein and the half pass back to the long side: this asks for greater bend with active outside aids, keeping the shoulder to the fore.
- Travers – half pirouette on the centre line – then half pass: increases collection, sensitivity and attentiveness.
- Half pass to the quarter line – shoulder-in straight – half pass – extend: demands submissiveness and balance.
- Half pass – ride straight on briskly – shoulder-fore – half pass – straight on: this varied work keeps the head clear and won't overstress the horse's muscles.

encourage the horse to take larger steps and gradually increase the difficulty. Throw in a figure of eight to break up the exercise.

- Spiral in on the circle almost in travers and then out again in a shoulder-in-like position, remembering to keep the horse moving on forwards: this asks for greater bend and collection and is good preparation for canter.
- Alternate shoulder-in and half pass with and without voltes in between: this will improve balance and increase suppleness.

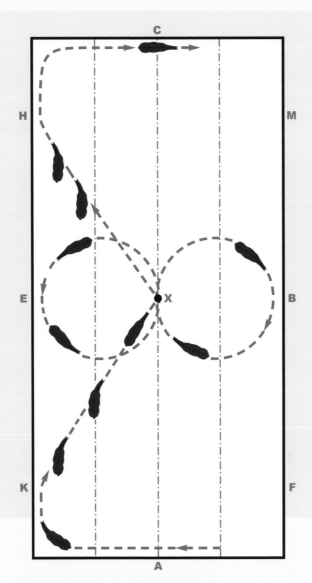

Two half passes to the centre line and back with a figure of eight over X.

- Half pass – volte – half pass: helps to check and improve bend but it is important for the rider to sit up straight and no collapse through the hip.
- Half pass to the quarter line (5 metre line) and back again (to E/B) then ride two half 10m circles changing rein over X: it is important to maintain a balanced quiet seat, with positive use of tension through the body, practising in short bursts. Keep the horse motivated.
- Half pass to the centre line and back again in canter (can be combined with a volte at X) with flying change: this demands a fast series of aids given and it is vital that the horse is

Right half pass with a good forwards rhythm.

kept in front of the seat. The horse has to go straight and the flying change allowed through. After changing rein ride a half halt and use the new outside rein and leg strongly to ask for the new half pass or volte, keeping the shoulder leading. If the horse is flexible and supple it responds to the rider's aids willingly and can be easily formed.

When you reach the stage of working on lateral movements you will then have at your disposal a huge wealth of gymnastic exercises now open to you, thus making any lesson more creative and interesting. Teamwork between horse and rider is essential. An understanding of the horse's mind and the capacity of the horse's body for work, keeping in mind its training programme, is a necessity and effective.

My tips for success

In all lateral movements there is a risk of confusing a horse moving over correctly with a horse whose quarters are moving across incorrectly due to its natural one-sidedness. This will only happen on one rein and is a sure sign that the horse wasn't going straight. Only when it can go straight, can a horse be evenly bent to both sides. If this isn't the case, then the horse is weak or stiff on one side and you will need to go back and work on straightness, remembering always to ride the horse

on forwards. All problems and weaknesses are caused by mistakes committed when doing the basics. You need to go back to the basics to improve these points and "erase" the errors. You don't do lateral movements just for the sake of doing them!

If you have worked through the basic training correctly, then you should start lateral work as soon as you can, as the structured nature of this work is the goal you are aiming at. The path to achieving paces that are actively forward-going, have plenty of impulsion, and are expressive, is a long one!

A horse with an active mind that works with you is an important prerequisite for being able to have fun when working on lightness in collection. Don't forget to always work in short bursts and alternate between collected and straightening paces. Only this will bring you success. Don't forget to take a break at the right moment after an exercise has worked well. In the canter work I tend to avoid riding too much travers and renvers. Due to the nature of the canter the horse tends to prefer avoiding taking up so much weight through the inside hind leg. It is only when working towards canter pirouette that canter work on travers and renvers on the circle is really called for. This helps to get the horse used to this very collected exercise and builds up the muscles required. The rider needs to pay attention that the horse stays in front of the seat and sits back on the hind legs, otherwise the quarters will move sideways without the necessary forwards movement.

It is important that the horse continues to enjoy the lateral work so that they are prepared to respond to the smallest of aids and continue to enjoy the simplicity of the exercise. The lateral movements can be used in a multitude of variations to form a creative training programme.

Collection perfected

Training a horse is a very interesting and varied process, the cornerstones of which are teamwork, harmony, discipline (especially of the rider!) and combined enjoyment in the work. The reward for this work is a long and an all in all healthy cooperation and a happy and expressive horse.

Dressage should be aimed at showing off a horse's beauty and elegance and allowing it to shine. This might be through a collected canter, a piaffe or canter to halt transition.

Depending on the horse's physical and mental ability, its training will take as long as necessary. The length of time isn't important. What is important is that the focus of training isn't on achieving the most movements in the shortest possible time, since this can increase the likeli-

hood of lameness or joint problems and, at worse, can even lead to the horse being unrideable.

The number of well-trained older horses that are used as schoolmasters shows that taking time is worth it. The training of such horses is done in such a way as to ensure that what is learned, stays learned. The rider will know when an aid has been applied correctly as the horse will respond and carry out the movement willingly and easily. The horse gives the rider a clear feedback!

Remember that all of the movements and exercises that follow need to be ridden in a high degree of collection and are easy to do and demand no particular strength.

The two factors of teamwork and staying fit and healthy are mutually reliant!

The collected canter: schooling canter

Not every rider has the chance to strengthen and build his horse's musculature by hacking out, jumping or using swimming pools or spas. It is important, therefore, to know how to achieve a round and even uphill canter without these tools.

Training towards collected canter – also known in Germany as schooling canter – is based on the work done in working canter. It takes time to prepare the horse's muscles, ligaments and tendons for the collected canter. This is the same as a skier preparing correctly in his training to be able to hit the slopes every day. Just like human athletes, horses also need a sensibly structured training plan that prepares them for the exercises involving more collection.

When a horse is particularly willing and enjoys its work, it is particularly important to know when to stop. If we chose the wrong moment and canter for too long "on the spot", this can lead to straining the back and joints. What was an attractive picture will be lost and the movement will become mechanical and forced. Instead of little strength being used, stronger and harder aids will be required.

Before you can ride a very collected canter the horse will need to be prepared for collection for weeks, months and years. The result of this basic work is that the horse will be able to work with a loose and swinging back in all paces and be able to carry itself in all of the movements learnt. It will be able to canter both in the corners and in counter canter with elastic movement with good impulsion. The lightest aid – almost as if by telepathy – should suffice to transition down, turn or extend the stride – this is the best way of checking the degree to which the horse is collected and on the aids.

In a correctly collected canter the rider should have a feeling of sitting on a forward-going horse. Its fluidity of movement and its lightness, combined with the collection, should minimise the level of aids that are required. The rider should only have to think about what he wants, for the horse to do it. This epitomises a harmonious and willing rider and horse partnership.

A supple horse that knows how to use its strength rationally will be a long-term and sound partner at the side of its rider.

It seems to me that increasingly fewer know how collected canter should correctly be ridden. There seems to be a real misunderstanding of what collection is. There is real benefit in learning what collection is as it will prove beneficial in the preparation for half pass, pirouettes or flying changes. The musculature of the back and quarters will be improved and it will allow the entire hind quarters to work as a giant spring. It will store and then release greater energy into the extensions.

A correctly collected canter on a straight line will show a clear flexion through the hocks with the horse lifting its legs through dynamically but gaining little forward movement in terms of the length of the stride. What should look like an impressive canter is marked by its energy, self-carriage and, of course, collection. On a straight line the inside hind leg comes down on a line that

Collected canter must be established before every movement. Advanced movements will then come more easily. Photo: Tierfotografie Huber.

lies between the fore legs, with the outside hind remaining under the centre of gravity. This helps to increase the ability of the horse to turn and the canter itself will clearly make less noise.

The rider catches the forward movement of the hind legs through his seat and back by sitting up straight and quiet. His hand remains soft and closes and holds the canter. The rider's quiet seat with a deeper knee allows the horse and rider appear as one.

A rider must always be able to recognise what his horse can do, based on both his horse's age and traininglevel. This and not the rider's ability should determine what training is done.

Collection is taken into the extension

My tips for success

Take small steps and avoid over-training or punishing the horse when things don't go right, so that the horse remains motivated and wants to work with you. The fastest and longest lasting progress is always made when there are no backwards steps!

There is always interaction between collection and extension, so don't forget to alternate between the two when training. Changing the tempo and taking breaks will help your horse to recover and relax its muscles as well as giving it a mental break. Ride fewer but better repetitions!

Canter pirouette

The pirouette is an expression of the highest level of collection and is where the quarters and the forehand each move on a circle. I have already detailed how they are ridden in earlier chapters. At this point we should be working on the perfection of the aids and the ability of the horse to carry itself.

After working on collected canter the horse can be prepared for pirouettes. The horse should be able to allow the impulsion through its body from back to the front and can be brought back and turned with the lightest of aids. Extension can be ridden out of the pirouette at any time thanks to the energy built up in the horse's body and the way the horse sits back and collects during the pirouette.

The expression and the elegance shown by horses in this movement is unique. The horse is moved with its forehand around its hind quarters in six stages, with the shoulder always slightly

The canter pirouette is an expression of the highest level of collection and requires the rider to be secure in her aids.
Photo: Tierfotografie Huber

leading. There should always be clear canter strides to be seen. There should be little movement forwards so that the horse looks as if it is cantering on the spot, but should always remain in front of the rider's seat. Self-carriage, balance and suppleness should be maintained throughout.

The rider should have a good but light contact and be able to end the pirouette at any stage and ride on in whatever tempo wished.

I will detail here a number of steps that can be worked through as you work towards the pirouette, which increase in difficulty as you work through them:

- Working pirouette from demi-pirouette or coming out of spiralling in and out on the circle.
- Quarter or eighth pirouettes in a square in short bursts with breaks in between.
- Demi-pirouette on a circle, riding on in counter canter and then back again.
- Demi pirouette on the diagonal.
- Full pirouette correctly ridden at any point in the manege. If rhythm, impulsion or balance is lost then ride forwards in extended canter. Stay relaxed and start over again, remembering to enjoy it when you get it right.

The correct combination of rider's aids is an indispensable prerequisite of a successful pirouette. Rapid but quietly effective aids offer the best support for a horse. Depending on the horse's nature, the pirouette may be ridden with the horse deeper or with a raised forehand. It is important, though, to maintain suppleness and relaxation throughout. It is always important to work according to the scales of training in all aspects of the movement. If there are any weaknesses then it is here that they will show. When show jumping it is never wise to go over jumps set to the same height all the time. It is better to jump lots of smaller obstacles to loosen up and gymnasticise the horse and avoid wear and tear.

The same applies to pirouette work. Lots of small steps will yield success! A well ridden pirouette places great demands on horse and rider and is a good indication of the level of training that a horse has reached.

The same applies to working on pirouettes: don't practice a hundred times, but rather recognise the weak spots and work on these.

Tempi changes

I have already written about the single flying change in canter. When we start to work on tempi changes – in other words, flying changes done with a given number of strides (or none) between each change – then the rider has "to learn to count". In addition, he has to be able to have a good feeling for the rhythm. Anyone who can dance (particularly ballroom or latin!) shouldn't have any problems counting when doing tempi changes and should be able to ride a series of changes one after the other. This really is a "good mood" exercise for both horse and rider.

To prepare for tempi changes the collected canter has to be secure. If the collected canter is ridden correctly, then the horse will be straight and in balance. It will be in self-carriage and uphill in its movement.

The rider must have really absorbed and memorised the aids required for the flying change, since they follow in very quick succession. The aids should have been so refined that the horse responds sensitively and responds easily to the canter aid. Tempi changes help both horse and rider to improve reaction time, coordination and the dynamics of the partnership.

One of the most important points to concentrate on when training tempi changes is the absolute straightness of the canter needed before, during and after the flying changes. The collected canter needs to be established without any loss in impulsion and with the horse "uphill". After the flying change the rider has to think of fluidly riding on without rushing. He has to concentrate on keeping a balanced seat as this helps to maintain the horse's balance. Once the horse is established in its changes, it should be able to do them on both straight lines and circles.

When it comes to tempi changes, count aloud! The stages to work through are:

1. Ride lots of single flying changes on straight lines, combining them together but without counting – in working and counter canter.
2. a: Try riding two to three three time changes one after another.

   b: Do several three time changes in a row.
3. Work on four time changes – at the start you should be happy with three or four sequences.
4. Riding two time changes, where there is only one canter stride between each change, requires you to keep the horse together and with a degree of tension through its body. Never change the horse's bend, as to do this would risk losing both balance and the straightness of the canter.
5. One time changes: follow the same principles as detailed above: start by doing fewer but straight changes. Then gradually ask for more one time changes, but remember to change the rein often. If you lose impulsion stop and ride forwards – remember, it is supposed to be fun and relax!

The aids for one time changes are as follows: the rider should have both calves behind the girth and in preparation presses lightly with the calf in time with the canter on the side that is going to be changed to. He then opens the leg to let the change through while, at the same time, the other leg is held still to contain the horse. This warns of the new change and then lets it through and then it starts all over again.

As the horse is in the suspended phase of the change, the aids for the next change is given. The rider needs to sit balanced and with an upright and quiet upper body. The hips and pelvis need to be kept quiet but loose and moves to the inside to lead the change.

> Don't throw yourself around in the saddle and don't wave your legs back and forth! Only then will your horse stay mentally and physically balanced!

You can't do tempi changes without having a good seat. The rider's aids should be virtually invisible to any spectator. If the horse is ridden rhythmically with well applied aids and good counting then there should be no problems in teaching a horse to do a series of changes. Here, too, it is a case of practice makes perfect!

At the conclusion, the rider needs to sit up, bring the forehand back in front of the quarters and ride on into a good canter without losing collection.

The point of this exercise is not only to compete at high levels in competition but equally to perfect your riding ability. Multiple flying changes require true cooperation between horse and rider.

Collected trot

I would venture to suggest that all riders think that they have at some stage ridden a collected trot. I will leave it up to you to form your own opinion as whether it was the same as what I am about to describe in the following section.

The collected trot can be recognised by the fact that it meets all of the points on the scales of training (rhythm, suppleness, contact, impulsion, straightness and collection). These will have all been systematically built up without causing the horse either mental or physical harm.

As a result of the mutual trust that forms between horse and rider during training, a picture of elegance and of a willing partnership will emerge. This can be seen in a horse that works happily with rhythmic paces, swinging through the back into the hand and is in self-carriage.

Training that builds further on this foundation leading to other collected movements will show a horse that has an easy elegance and confident movement. The more correct that this trot is ridden, the less obvious will the aids be. A horse that is ridden slightly IN FRONT of the vertical will gain in expression and appeal.

A horse that really swings through its back and is relaxed and supple in both mind and body, that appears to move happily through its world with an elevated outline, will always be ready for high performance.

The horse will almost be showing the first signs of the passage since the movement is elevated and light. It is therefore never difficult to move in and out of collection into extended trot, lateral movements or even piaffe and passage. During the transitions, the horse should stay in front of the rider's seat and will give him a feeling of regularity of rhythm and impulsion. Too much hand is definitely out of place here!

Once the horse is securely on the aids then even transitions with the reins held in one hand should be possible.
Photo: Tierfotografie Huber

Once you have experienced the swinging movement of the collected trot, then you know what correct riding is all about!

In the back of his mind, the rider should always remember that the horse can't sit down for a break, so it is the rider's job to use the dressage exercises to keep his horse healthy, build up the horse's self-confidence, as well as making the horse both prouder and more beautiful. If you don't think that you have any use for the described collected trot for competitions, then think again. Learning to ride and teaching a rhythmical collected trot has not yet gone out of fashion, especially since not all horses naturally have an elastic trot.

Working in-hand and half steps

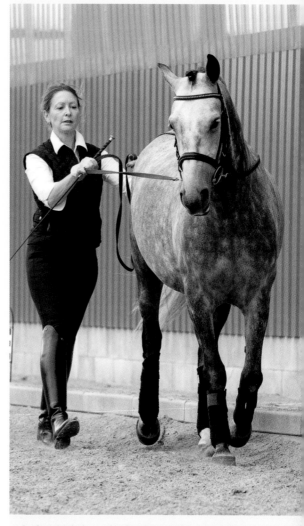

In the initial phase of in-hand training, here using long reins, the aids and rhythm should be worked on.

Teaching in hand has many advantages since it helps to develop trust and communication between horse and rider. You will now graduate from primary work to secondary school!

The horse's suppleness, lateral movements and collection can all be developed and fostered by working in hand. Because of the huge variety of possibilities that exist when working in hand, I will limit myself here to using it for developing collection.

In hand work is the foundation for the work that comes later in piaffe and passage. In the initial phase when getting the horse used to the work

in hand, the aids will need to be established and the rhythm controlled. The hind legs will be brought through underneath a rounded back, ensuring that the back is optimally relieved. The handler will have a light and elastic contact through the reins. Using shoulder-fore the horse will be kept straight and by changing the rein frequently the inside hind leg will be stretched and suppled. Work on collection can now begin.

All collected movements can be prepared and developed using in-hand work

My tips for success

The work in hand which I find fascinating demands a degree of sensitivity and structure in its execution. Always ask yourself critically when problems arise who made the mistake first and when! Ninety-nine percent of the time it isn't the horse that is disobedient, but it is more likely that the rider has made a basic mistake in communication, such as not asking in the right way. As long as you are aware of where you stand yourself in your training, the horse will follow you as far as possible. Over-training and mental confusion lead to long-term damage in the ability of a horse to learn and carry out the exercise.

Don't just practice the main exercise we are talking about here (the piaffe on page 121) but, at the same time work, on the sequence of steps in the half steps, the transitions from or into walk or trot. Even a few, small half steps should be recognised and praised. Use the relaxation that moving on into trot from collection offers, a transition to walk in shoulder-fore – a short break – or a halt. All of this can be sweetened with praise and a reward so that the horse is positively conditioned.

Working in hand offers a variety of other possibilities to maintain lightness. You can use the transition from trot into walk to practice shortening and collecting and ask for a few half steps. Stretching, flexing through the poll and neck, and allowing the horse to take the contact down all help to improve suppleness. Never forget to praise!

The biggest reward that a horse can be given is a break between exercises to allow the horse to process what it has done and to allow what has been learnt to sink in. Here, too, the principle of "less is more" applies. Start with only a few minutes of work. Later, you can work through exercises every day, but always be satisfied with a few steps.

Stopping at the right time will keep the horse motivated and will succeed faster and without force!

Piaffe and Passage

As already indicated, when you look at horses of mixed ages and mixed level of training out in the field, you will very quickly see that they can already carry out all the movements that we think that we need to teach them. It is fun to observe the ease with which they move. Then the long journey begins to train them with the rider on their back and to teach them balance, suppleness, motivation and lightness in all of the movements.

All of the steps detailed up until now are necessary parts of this training journey to reach the final destination. The journey is the reward when training your horse to an advanced level and maintaining this attitude will help to keep a horse motivated along the way. When a horse, either young or being retrained, and rider have progressed far enough that they can execute piaffe, then you will see that all of the previous chapters have been the stepping stones towards this.

Competitions serve to test what has been learnt. This means that horses that are trained to elementary compete at novice, to medium compete at elementary and the horses that are trained to

Intermediare I should compete at Prix St George. Especially when in a new environment it is sensible to ask for the movements that you know a horse is good at and confident in performing so that too much isn't being asked. By doing this you will avoid setbacks. Training should be done at home, not when out competing!

Anyone who has read this far knows that training takes time: It requires a high level of performance from a horse to develop the ability to carry itself enough that it is able to move on the spot. Compare this to some riders who have been heard to say "If my four-year-old doesn't piaffe, then I won't continue training it, since it isn't talented enough for Grand Prix". When I hear statements like this I wonder who is lacking in talent!

Piaffe

When we see a good piaffe that has been established over time – recognisable by the ease of movement and its uphill tendency – then we are very close to reaching the pinnacle of a horse's training. It is a first class stamp of quality.
The piaffe is prepared for and taught by:
1. Carefully working through transitions with the hind quarters being engaged and regular and rhythmic stepping of the hind legs. The balance of weight between the forehand and hind quarters should be 1:3.
2. Getting a horse used to working in hand.
3. Working in hand in small bursts, repeating daily before riding.
4. Piaffe in hand, allowing some forwards movement and then trot on.
5. Riding in piaffe but alternate with other movements, such as half pass, pirouette or extensions.

Piaffe demands a high level of performance from a horse. The strength required for the horse to carry its weight through its quarters requires years of preparation. Photo: Tierfotografie Huber

Some fundamental characteristics of the piaffe:
- Greater bending of the haunches whilst maintaining energy through the hind legs.
- Relaxed but contained back (acting as a bridge between the quarters and the forehand around the horse's centre of gravity)
- Optimal freedom through the shoulder with an accentuated lifting of the forelegs.

Over time I have established that it is effective to remind my horses of the work facing them by working them in hand before I get on them. I go through the individual training steps methodically, warming the horse up while at the same time engaging the hocks so they step well underneath the horse.

In doing this, it is important, though, that you don't ask too much too soon, but instead work according to the horse's stage of training.

This gymnastic work in hand allowing slightly forwards, offers relief to the horse's back and helps the muscles to strengthen in the right places, thereby protecting the horse from the risk of strain and overwork.

Riding is the greatest example of teamwork between rider and horse coming from an upright, relaxed seat – virtually from a deeply relaxed and emotional connection of horse and rider. Horses can perceive a person's aura. You will have noticed this, from when you have gone to ride when either in a rush or in a bad mood. The horse will back off or is inattentive and doesn't take you seriously. They are a mirror of ourselves.

When working in hand and when under saddle, the piaffe sensitises the horse greatly. The aids are refined more and more until the horse can be directed just by pointing. This movement teaches the rider just how lightly aids need to be applied, as it is only by carefully combining all of the aids that the right combination can be developed.

At the beginning of piaffe work it is important to have a good trainer who can help from the ground and support the training by applying minor but correct impulsive aids.

Serious mistakes can also be made here and which damage or even destroy the foundation of the basic work. The key is trust. This should never be put at risk by asking too much or for-

The piaffe is developed out of half steps. An instructor can offer support at the start.

cing a movement. Allow yourself and your horse time to understand the work fully.

If you try to force collection then there will always be negative consequences. Examples of problems that are caused and their solution are:

- Lazy steps, especially of the forehand: start the piaffe with the horse going more forwards. Ride trot-walk transitions with a few half steps in the transitions.
- The horse looks tense: work on suppleness and relaxedness, training in short bursts. Do less but then do it correctly.
- Irregular rhythm: go back to half steps in preparation for the piaffe. Always work forwards.
- The hindquarters lower too much and impulsion is lost from the hind legs, shuffling: train with less bend through the haunches, ride lots of transitions asking for only a few piaffe steps and then into trot.
- The hind legs lift up too much and the horse falls on its forehand: work forwards in shoulder-fore, use your whip higher on the croup as if you want to trot on. Always pay attention to the balance between the forehand and the hind quarters. It is important that the horse remains active and doesn't creep back.
- Resistance: analyse where the resistance is coming from. What has gone wrong? Go back through the individual training steps and start again. Check that the horse is relaxed, supple and straight by allowing the horse to take the contact down on a long rein. Don't clock up the miles – in other words, don't train too much or for too long.

All difficulties usually come from progressing too quickly through a horse's training. If you proceed with caution and concentrate on the basics with young horses, then horse and rider will have many years of learning and training in front of them to prepare correctly for the piaffe.

A horse may appear to offer small piaffe steps early on but these can be deceptive and don't guarantee that the horse will later be able to do a correct piaffe, that can be performed whenever asked.

A rider that can correctly utilise his horse's power will have saved energy for all of the other movements and can then use this for the training sessions that follow. It is important to build in breaks: even if it is just bringing the horse to a square halt and pausing for a moment. The "throughness" of the horse from its quarters through to the forehand is captured through the rider's quiet seat and turns into an almost trot-like movement on the spot. You should constantly remind yourself that the most important aim of this exercise is to supple the horse and turn it into a healthy athlete.

A particular highlight of this movement is smoothly riding the transitions into and out of the piaffe – an exercise that really does demand a lot physically from the horse. If the horse manages to do it then it is a wonderful feeling, since you can feel the horse's submissiveness and flexibility throughout its entire body.

What is decisive is the understanding that art only works in harmony with nature and with the horse's physiology; otherwise, it isn't art!

No movement stands alone, but rather is a part of the whole. For this reason piaffe makes up one component of a horse's entire education. I start the initial work on piaffe early on in my training programme. The work done on simple transitions is ideal for this: the shortening through the frame that trot-walk transitions demand represents the shortening asked in the initial stages of piaffe and comes very close to the half steps I have already detailed, feeling very similar. It is only when the horse can carry out piaffe easily and can go from it into another movement with ease, that we can say we are riding the movement with the correct degree of collection.

Variations
- Walk – piaffe – demi pirouette
- Walk – piaffe – medium trot – halt
- Trot – piaffe – halt
- Trot – piaffe – trot
- Canter – demi pirouette – piaffe – medium trot
- Shoulder-in – demi pirouette with piaffe-like steps – renvers
- Centre line – trot – Piaffe – half pass
- Ride E-B – walk – Piaffe – walk – demi pirouette – walk – piaffe – walk

Ride piaffe exercises firstly on the outside track, using the outside of the school or manege to support you, before trying to ride away from the track. At the start of piaffe work ask for only a few steps and try to keep a degree of lightness.

Stay creative when putting together your training exercises and carefully consider the age, conformation and temperament of the horse. The more advanced collection becomes, the less hand and rein will be required.

Passage

When working on passage which demands a high degree of impulsion and carrying power of the hind legs, it is important that the horse remains compact.

Passage should only be asked for after piaffe can be done well, even if the conformation of today's modern sport horses appear to allow for this work being started much faster. Trot-like steps with a lot of elevation and cadence have nothing in common with true passage. You shouldn't be fooled by this, as you will pay for it later. Once a horse has learnt to do something incorrectly, getting it to "unlearn" it can be very problematic. Usually, it isn't just the forehand that is put under too much strain, in other words, the balance between the forehand and hind quarters isn't right, but also to a certain extent the back, that can't fulfil its role as a bridge between the two.

Any horse that has a particular talent for passage will always be able to fulfil this potential following appropriate training. It never loses this talent, just as a particularly talented showjumper never loses its ability to jump. In the latter case, daily riding over very high jumps can, however, lead to injury and unnecessarily early wear and tear. It is exactly the same with passage, if too much is done and in the wrong way.

You can practice hitting a golf ball from the tee thousands of times and refine your swing. A horse will quickly grow tired of this type of training, becoming stubborn and resistant so that

Impulsion and the carrying power of the haunches are what really distinguish the passage. Photo: Tierfotografie Huber

any further productive work can be forgotten about.

If you can develop passage out of a good uphill piaffe then it gives you the security of knowing that you will be able to ride it from any movement. A correctly trained passage has to fulfil the same criteria as the piaffe: balance, freedom of the forehand, appropriate lifting of the hind legs as well as impulsion while moving forwards with cadence but with an extended moment of suspension. It doesn't demand as much collection as with the piaffe however. Particular attention has to be placed on the coordination of the thrust coming from behind and the flexion of the haunches so that the perfection of the trot can be reached with power and cadence.

After working in piaffe the horse can be led into the passage. This is also possible from collected trot. Here, though, you need to be a very good rider, aware of how and where aids are given in order to maintain the correct sequence of hand-seat-leg. The safest way is to start from walk, using all of the movements in varying combinations as follows:

- Piaffe – passage – extended trot
- Walk – passage – piaffe
- Extended trot – passage – canter
- Piaffe – passage – piaffe

In a correct passage-piaffe transition the rider should sit deep, quiet and upright on the horse, applying only minimal aids.

Today in international competitions, instead of the truly classical passage you see more passage with little bend of the haunches, but going much more forwards. This then results in problems that can often be seen: the horse is supposed to be collected back into piaffe from an incorrect passage which is possibly unbalanced (the balance of the hind quarters to the forehand is 1:1 instead of 3:1), has little bend through the haunches and is lacking in impulsion and lightness. It won't be able to do a transition into piaffe, collected canter or halt. In addition, when the horse is having problems because it has lost its balance, then the rider will not be able to do it without using a lot of hand – and this causes more weight to come onto the forehand which is not only wrong, but bad for the horse.

This will lead to all the previous, successfully learnt transitions suffering as well. In the worst cases, you may need to call for a physio to treat the tension that will have built up in the back and neck of both horse and rider. It is only when the horse's body is totally mobile that the full range of its movements be made use of.

My tips for success

With all collected work you always need to remember that you are your horse's fitness trainer and you need to design a new gymnastic programme for it every day that will benefit its entire body. By concentrating on only one part, for example, only on the quarters or on the forehand, it will be to the detriment of the fluidity of it movement and suppleness. Be satisfied initially with smaller and perhaps less spectacular movements and pay attention that the horse's centre of gravity and self-carriage are always maintained. Only from this can a horse really develop its expression.

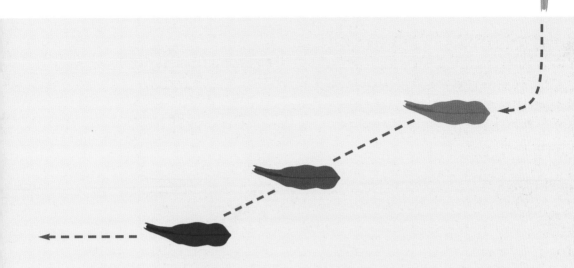

Training programme

In the previous chapters we have gone through a succession of lessons that have worked from easier to harder movements, offering a single thread that links all elements of a horse's training. Now I am going to put together appropriate training plans for your horse using these exercises and movements.

A horse's life has different phases. It begins with the horse starting work when it is backed and going through its novice phase. The training from six to ten years is the most intensive time for training. From ten, the rider should be able to take advantage of the horse's training and ride the full range of movements. For the older horse the focus should be on working on individual movements and maintaining its musculature always after being correctly warmed up. For this

reason, a training plan has to be individually designed according to the ability of the rider, the potential of the horse, its age, level of training, temperament and its ability to learn.

First of all, you need to establish where you are with your horse, then start from where its training is up to.

This book represents an introduction to training with the most important basics for putting together a training programme. You are your horse's trainer and when you are familiar with the fundamental principles and problems you will be better able to construct varied daily, weekly and monthly training programmes.

First of all, though, you need to check exactly where you are. The main questions to ask are: is the horse coming off my seat and on the aids? Do horse and rider speak in the same language? In particular, this means:

• Is the horse accepting driving legs aids that are being correctly applied on one side and from both sides?

• Does the horse respond to the seat and weight aids immediately, or does it take time to think about it first?

• Is the contact with the horse's mouth elastic and soft, do the hand and the mouth seek the contact and does the rider use his seat to frame and contain the horse?

• Is the working atmosphere good and is there a positive environment to work in?

At every stage of training the horse needs to understand what the rider wants from it:

It is particularly important for training if it is to be successful that the horse clearly understands what it is being asked to do!

When there are misunderstandings you have to first of all ask yourself:

• Have I done something wrong? Did I apply my aids in the right place, to the right degree and did my seat remain soft?

• Was what I asked my horse to do appropriate for its level of training and prepared for correctly?

• Did I structure the lesson logically?

• Answer these questions honestly and then try the exercise again.

Working in small steps

You can only avoid the risk of asking too much of your horse by ensuring that you work in small easily understood steps. Make certain that you try to follow these guidelines:

• Get to know and understand the movement or exercise.

• Ride the exercise; initially, it doesn't have to be exact.

• Practice and refine the exercise.

• Change the rein often and repeat the exercise at different points around the manege.

• Ride different versions of the same exercise, for example, incorporating serpentines with voltes, and start to build in transitions from collected to extended paces.

Work on the circle using these guidelines could look like this:

• Start by riding on a square circle.

• Improve working on the circle on both reins, using eight to 16 corner circles.

• Be more exact in riding on the circle concentrating on achieving the right bend and flexion on a circle that is round.

• Ride in first or second position on a correctly shaped circle.

• Make certain that the circle is ridden with the horse's hind feet stepping around the circle correctly, as well as in first and second position, "walk on a beam", enjoy the cadence of the movement as well as the freedom through the shoulder that this gives you.

• Right different combinations using circles: voltes in shoulder-in, spiralling in and out, incorporating simple canter changes and counter canter. Always keep the horse in front of your seat!

Misunderstandings and how to deal with them

When you put together a training programme, it is important to recognise that your horse is an individual. Weaknesses that reoccur will have to be improved on and overcome by being creative in putting together exercises. Misunderstandings can happen – don't get stuck on one thing but try to instead work through them by varying your exercises and making them fun. Riding a variety of schooling figures and being creative will keep both you and your horse fresh, attentive and willing to learn.

Lesson planning

A horse's training needs to be structured and the contents planned both within the individual sessions and throughout its entire life.

Initial training starts by working on the following key points:

- Building trust, stretching and loosening up the horse.
- Using gymnastic exercises, a horse, that is moving straight, will improve its fitness and mobility. At the same time, submission and impulsion coming from behind and back will start to be developed.
- In the third phase we need to improve the balance between the hind quarters and forehand using collected work. The horse's centre of gravity moves back towards the hind quarters. In doing so, exercises already learnt will be improved and refined.

Misunderstandings do happen – don't let them upset you!

- A training session should always be ended by repeating some of the basic exercises. The horse should always go relaxed on both long and short rein in balance and with active hind legs, without rushing. The horse should be happy to take the reins down and stretch and then allow them to be taken up again without losing rhythm. The single thread that I referred to above should be sewn into in every exercise at every stage of a horse's education. Every lesson should encompass ever more features of the scale of training like a spider's web. It is important for me, that I follow this thread stitch by stitch, or step by step, but answer the challenges that our horses pose us by thinking creatively.

My principles:
- Straighten then bend!
- Straighten your horse and then ride on forwards!
- Only start to ask for light collection when your horse can go straight and can bend.
- Use lateral work to get suppleness, throughness and freedom through the shoulder!
- Only bring a relaxed, flexible and straightened horse into true collection.

The "time table" for your daily training session consists of three stages. During the warm-up balance, rhythm and tempo should be established. To supple your horse in as short a time as possible use the pace that your horse finds easiest to work in. In this part of the basic work you should work on the horse's ability to stretch and flex, elastically taking up and giving the contact so the horse begins to work through and become more submissive. The ability of the horse to trust and accept the aids and the language between horse and rider should become more firmly established from day to day. The schooling figures should be ridden with carefully applied aids and concentration from day one. All of this gymnastic work at the start aim to improve the horse's coordination and fitness. Exercises have to be selected that suit the individual horse. In the second working phase, the horse will be straightened, impulsion developed and the carrying power of the quarters improved. The goal is to develop and improve greater freedom through the shoulder, cadence of pace and collection. Use your aids carefully. You should work on your horse's weak points every day, repeating exercises targeted at overcoming these weaknesses. Do this by starting with a familiar exercise and repeat, refine and then vary it. Work using short sessions so that training can move forward in small steps. Always end with something that the horse can do well so you end on a good note.

In the cool down, or relaxation phase, the horse should be mentally and physically relaxed using exercises from the basic phase of training. Check the horse's suppleness, always maintaining the balance, by allowing the horse to stretch down on a long rein. Using a correctly constructed training plan the horse should come back to its stable relaxed and supple so that next time you will have a contented horse that is ready for its next lesson. Every lesson should be fun when it is structured correctly and the horse knows what it should be learning next. Be sure that you give your horse clear direction and instruction.

Problem horses and weaknesses

If you have a horse that can't immediately be ridden to plan, look for what lies behind this, whether internal or exterior problems. A horse that is overdeveloped underneath his neck will need longer to relax and warm up. If a horse has

Horses with conformation issues such as a long back will need exercises designed just for them.

done too much as a youngster or has been treated badly then trust will need to be built up before you can really start to train.

Find out what difficulties you are going to be faced with. Solve them and put them to one side totally so that they don't keep re-emerging as you progress through your training. This saves time and energy for horse and rider later on!

I have often had to deal with horses in for corrective training that apparently have bad habits including being spooky, lazy or stubborn. The causes for being a difficult ride or for lameness can often easily be found by looking back at a horse's training and then going back to basics. If we start from the beginning again you will often see that, as if by a miracle, your "ugly duckling" becomes a beautiful swan as you work through your training, this time correctly.

The more a horse can move relaxed and in balance, the faster its flexibility and suppleness will improve. If a horse feels well in itself then its motivation to work will increase and it will move through its training much faster. The rider needs to set down a long-term training framework in which the horse can really blossom. Out of what was before an underperforming doormat, you will gain an enthusiastic and attentive new partner.

Only when you open your eyes and hone your senses will you able to attain the highest levels of riding.

Weekly plan

This weekly training plan can only be used with horses that are already well on their way! All other horses will need notably longer in their warm-up and cool down and you will also need to take it slower with them within a week. This may mean stretching a week's programme out over an entire month. As soon as you have established relaxed suppleness in all paces on both reins, then go back to the weekly plan. Have fun!

Monday: loosening work

We start daily with lots of walk before entering the manege. Then we begin the warm up in all of the paces, checking that the aids are being accepted and the horse's muscles are warmed up and prepared for the training to come. In the case of young horses or those in for retraining, we tend to only ride straight lines at first. With older horses we check briefly that they are on the aids and then move straight away onto proper work. Loosening exercises with changing bend and simple transition end the work phase. We end today's training by hacking out as long as time allows in walk.

Tuesday: intensive training

Start again in walk. Go over the suppling work from the day before, clearly asking for straightness. Work on a circle allowing the horse to stretch and take the rein down, zig zag serpentines, shoulder-fore or shoulder-in at walk, adding in demi pirouettes. Moving onto trot, check for straightness and bend. Ride simple transitions between all of the paces on circles and serpentines – do eight to ten transitions on each rein, changing the rein constantly. Now come the exercises targeted at improving specific weaknesses: improve the mobility of the back and its strength using transitions and lateral work, or use tempi changes in canter to work on submission. Wor-

	Mon	Tues
At least 10 mins walk	X	X
Warm-up + loosening	15 mins	10 mins
Rough versions	X	X
Refine the exercises		X
Variations		X
Lower level of performance intensity	X	
Require higher level of performance		X
Cool down	10 mins	5 mins
Ride at least 10 mins in walk and hack out on harder ground for 5 mins	20 mins	15 mins
Emphasis on	Loosening work	Intensive training

134

Wed	Thurs	Fri	Sat	Sun	Examples
X	X	X	X	X	Ride on centre line, diagonals and serpentines • Voltes • Lateral work • Demi-pirouette
5 mins	20 mins	10 mins	5 mins	5 mins	Canter and rising trot • Circles • Serpentines • Simple trot – canter • Lateral work
					Start to ride the targeted exercises or new movements.
X		X	X	X	Work more precisely on the exercises
X		X	X	X	Make the movements more automatic and vary them
X		X			Simple range of exercises as well as working on the targeted exercises or a new movement once or twice
	X		X	X	Ride targeted exercises 4 to 6 times for each one
5 mins	3 mins	5 mins	5 mins	10 mins	Change the rein and allow the horse to stretch and take the rein down on the circle and serpentines.
15 mins	20 mins	20 mins	20 mins	15 mins	Medium walk on a long rein using circles, serpentines or hacking out
Securing the exercises	Having fun	Intensive training	Playful work	Exactness, possible competition preparation	• Always work from the known to the unknown • Always go from easy to hard.

king in hand and on shoulder-in can improve a horse's collection and containment.

We can also start to prepare for the exercises that come later, using serpentines and riding in flexion to prepare for the shoulder-in, trot/canter-walk transitions for the halt or simple canter changes as preparation for the flying change. To end this more intensive training session we allow the horse to relax, but without letting it fall apart and go flat! This means allowing it to stretch down but not losing the engagement of the quarters. If the horse has truly been ridden off our seat using the correct aids then it should be able to be ridden relaxed with a longer neck without losing its balance. Finish the session by riding serpentines in walk on a long rein.

Wednesday: securing the exercises

Every horse is different: some need one day of hard work and then more relaxed training, others can cope with two consecutive days or harder training. We are assuming here that our horses are of the second type, therefore today we are building on the work of yesterday. After the warm-up and loosening phase, we go over the exercise we specifically worked on yesterday and start to refine it. Depending on the exercise you may want to ride, increase the difficulty. Pay attention, though, to polishing your work.

The horse's mental attitude will also guide you in your work. In the case of a horse that is less concentrated, you may want to work on the same thing as yesterday. With a horse that is more laid back and passive, a change of scene may help to keep up its motivation and concentration. Try hacking out or going to a different place to train.

Thursday: having fun

On Thursday after 10 minutes of walk we warm our horses up making sure their muscles are loose and supple and then we start with some easy work over cavaletti and small jumps. Loose schooling over jumps is a good alternative as well as this uses different muscle groups. You can still work on the exercises you have targeted for the week when out hacking or when jumping: In between, ask the horse to stretch down and work on straightness, for example, riding shoulder-fore in canter. Riding in walk is good for the muscles and for the mind! Use serpentines, leg yielding and allow the horse stretch and take the reins down in your cool down. Hacking out keeps the horse mentally alert and the uneven ground helps improve its sure-footedness.

Friday: intensive training

Today, too, we put a lot of emphasis on beginning in the walk. Think about straightness straight away. After riding the diagonals a few times in trot and canter move straight away onto circles to get the horse supple as quickly as possible. Build in transitions at the same time. This means we aren't wasting either time or energy and the horse will be much better prepared for the more strenuous work to follow. The aims for today may be the same as on Wednesday, checking that the horse remembers what it has been taught and trying new variations: shoulder-in alternating with medium trot, shoulder-in on the circle alternating with renvers or shoulder-in in canter with a half circle and back on the track, followed by counter canter on the circle. Don't forget about cooling off and stretching at the end and the final walk!

Saturday: playing with work

If your horse has worked well then it can be surprising how refreshing an easier day can be for both of you. Concentrate on asking for what has been learned during the week without confrontation and using the lightest of aids. We want the horse to have a totally positive experience today. We work along the same lines as on Friday in terms of the structure of the lesson but ask for less in terms of the level performance and the length of time.

Sunday: working on precision

If successful with yesterday's work then we start with more intensive work at walk in shoulder-in, travers and demi pirouettes. This is followed by 20 minutes of working more intensively on what has been done during the week. Ask for the movements to be clear on defined lines and correct. Ride shoulder-in on the circle two to three times and each time on each hand come out of the shoulder-in with either extended strides, or straighten and ask for one of the lateral movements. Everything that the horse enjoys doing can be ridden in many different combinations. Never lose the ease with which the movement is completed. We can see this by how well the horse accepts its rider's aids. End the session with canter in a forward seat, flying changes or several simple trot-canter-trot transitions. These, too, should come from the lightest of aids.

Using this model of training we have used every day of the week well. If the horses learn well and the riders don't make too many mistakes, I know from experience that working in smaller and shorter training sessions is more than enough. Children, too, depending on their age and maturity can't concentrate for much more than 30 – 45 minutes.

As is often quoted, "Less is more!" If you make mistakes that your horse mirrors, don't make it worse by getting upset or punishing it. Try it again but ride more effectively. There are always times during which your horse is coping with physical changes – such as when it is moulting, after inoculations or other down times.

During these times, training should be made easier. A horse's musculature shouldn't be put under additional strain when it is preoccupied with other things. If this happens then we don't have to just repair its muscles, but also probably its mind since it will remember being ridden with sore muscles for a long time. In this situation riders have to learn to find the right balance and learn from their mistakes. Only then will the horse trust the rider and his aids and rather than being an automaton that can technically perform the movements will become a enthusiastic, co-operative partner that is a joy for us to ride every day.

You will achieve the highest of performance with ease and whilst overcoming fears. This cooperation relies on mutual respect and trust.

A final word

The dressage training of horses is the basis of all riding activity and reaches its climax in lightness, expression and naturalness of movement. All of the exercises and movements that lead to that point represent a body-building programme so that the horse can carry the rider's weight. To do this, the horse needs a body that is fit, strong, fast and skilled, without suffering wear and tear. Based on a healthy body with sufficiently developed muscles and mental agility the horse will be able to carry out the movements we ask of it correctly with the minimum of aids. Our sporting partner, the horse, will thank us with long- lasting health and a long life.

It isn't just physical fitness, but mental attitude, too, is of great significance. "There is

strength in calmness" – we shouldn't just think of this saying for the sake of our horses. Our relationship with horses should be based on calmness and mutual respect. It is our goal to maintain not just their mental equilibrium over the long term, but also their motivation and health. If we deal with our horses with clear thoughts, an alert mind and a calm attitude then we will achieve astonishing results. Every one of our movements involves body language and thus communication with our horses. Remember that learning is all about positive conditioning so it is important that you create a lasting atmosphere of trust and cooperation. This will work by using a long-term training plan based on mutual respect and teamwork. For the rider, this means preparing correctly for the dressage work and planning systematically ahead. "A good rider knows precisely why he is riding a particular movement and giving particular aids."

Having come to the end of this book, I would like to thank all of those who worked with me on it and wish you much enjoyment in developing your new training programme. And always remember: no one is born an expert.

Index

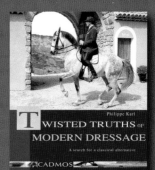
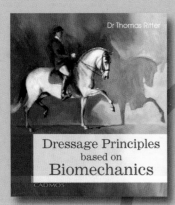

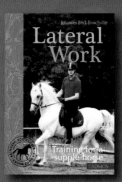